NO
PERMANENT
CITY

NO PERMANENT CITY

Stories from Mennonite History and Life

HARRY LOEWEN

HERALD PRESS
Waterloo, Ontario
Scottdale, Pennsylvania

Canadian Cataloguing in Publication Data
Loewen, Harry, 1930-
   No permanent city : stories from Mennonite history and life.

Includes bibliographical references.
ISBN 0-8361-3612-8

1. Mennonites—History. 2. Anabaptists—History. 3. Mennonites—Social
life and customs. 4. Anabaptists—Social life and customs. I. Title.

BX8115.L74 1993   289.7'09   C92-094922-3

The paper used in this publication is recycled and meets the minimum re-
quirements of American National Standard for Information Sciences—
Permanence of Paper for Printed Library Materials, ANSI Z39.48-1984.

Grateful acknowledgment is made for permission to use art from the files
of Jan Gleysteen on pp. 52, 64, 87, 120; on p. 192 from Dietrich Neufeld, *A
Russian Dance of Death: Revolution and Civil War in the Ukraine,* trans.
from the German and ed. Al Reimer (Winnipeg: Hyperion Press, 1977).

Reproduction on p. 28 is from the spine of a book by Joseph von Lauff,
Elisabeth Wandscherer die Königin. Roman (Leipzig: Verlag von K. F.
Koehler, 1931); on p. 71 is from T. J. v. Bracht's *Märtyrer-Spiegel,*
Lewistown, Pa.: Shem Zook, printed at Philadelphia: King & Baird, 1849.

Drawings on pp. 22, 47, 140, 155, 169, 205 by Gwen M. Stamm.

NO PERMANENT CITY
Copyright © 1993 by Herald Press, Waterloo, Ont. N2L 6H7
   Published simultaneously in the United States by Herald Press,
   Scottdale, Pa. 15683. All rights reserved
Library of Congress Catalog Number: 92-73439
International Standard Book Number: 0-8361-3612-8
Printed in the United States of America
Book and cover design by Paula M. Johnson/Cover art by Arthur L. Sprunger;
used by permission of Rebecca Sprunger Wetzel

1 2 3 4 5 6 7 8 9 10 99 98 97 96 95 94 93

*This book is dedicated to
my Catholic-Mennonite children,
Charles and Dana Loewen, who are
diligently teaching my grandchildren,
Brent and Amber, a faith and
way of life derived from the
Catholic and Anabaptist-
Mennonite traditions.*

Contents

Preface and Acknowledgments

*T*he main title of this collection
of stories, *No Permanent City*, hints at the struggle Mennonites
originally had in finding places in which to settle. In the beginning
of their history, Anabaptists and Mennonites faced persecution, exile, and violation of their rights as citizens of countries or territories
in which they sought to live according to conscience.

In time, however, they were received and tolerated by rulers who
profited economically from Mennonites' thrift and hard work as
tenants, farmers, craftsmen, business people, and professionals.
Mennonites themselves began to acquire land and status and eventually became prosperous. As landholders and respected citizens,
they developed a way of life which often did not resemble their
humble beginnings. Ironically, as is shown in "Whose Land?" a
story whose theme relates to that of the title story, Mennonites in
their search for a homeland sometimes displaced native peoples.

The stories in this book deal with the early beginnings of the
Anabaptist-Mennonites and their later history and life throughout
the world. These accounts are not intended to teach moral lessons
but to entertain and to inform the reader concerning aspects of
Mennonite faith and life.

The stories are historically true rather than fictional in that most
are placed within their historical setting and significance. However,
some stories are more "historical" than others, while a few are hu-

man interest tales from Mennonite life. Such stories as "The Canary," "A Love Story," or "The First Train Ride," for example, may resemble fiction or fictionalized accounts. They are, however, based on actual experiences and often portray or reflect Mennonite cultural life better than a historical account.

To give the reader a sense of historical development, I have arranged the stories more or less chronologically, beginning with the Anabaptists of the sixteenth century and concluding with stories set in our time. There are stories from the rich Anabaptist heritage; stories from Mennonite history in the European countries, including Switzerland, the Netherlands, Germany, Prussia, and Russia; and stories dealing with Mennonites in the United States, Canada, and South America. The last few selections draw on some of my own experiences and ideas, thus providing a contemporary flavor of Mennonite life.

No story appears in completely original form. I selected stories from archival materials, unpublished manuscripts and published books and articles. Then I reworked, adapted, and retold them for this book. Some stories required extensive reading and research, such as "The Spear of the Moros" and "The Story of Christian Funk." Others I found ready-made, as it were, for adaptation and retelling. The popular English style in which the stories are written should make them accessible to readers in all walks of life.

My approach to history in this volume is narrative rather than analytical and interpretive, although even a storyteller reflects on the events recounted. The stories of a people not only foster that people's collective memory but also help that people's individuals and communities identify with their culture, faith, and spiritual heritage. Those with special interests will read scholarly journals and books, but many more people will want to read stories about their past and learn through them their history as a people. I hope the stories presented here will help readers to a better understanding of the Mennonite people and reflection on their faith and practice.

This book could not have been written without the help of many persons and institutions. Gary Waltner, director of the Mennonitische Forschungsstelle at the Weierhof, Germany, assisted me with the resources of his archival centre. Through the kind hospitality of Peter Foth and his family, I found access to the old and well-stocked library of the Mennonite Church of Hamburg-Altona, Germany.

Gudrun Harder and her daughter-in-law Christine Böhm kindly took me in their car to the beautiful Geisberg castle south of Wissembourge, France. Diether Götz Lichdy of Heilbronn, Germany, provided valuable details concerning the Mennonites of the Palatinate. While in Germany I lodged in a guest residence of the University of Mannheim, where Kurt-Friedrich Bohrer did his best to make my stay as pleasant as possible.

While working on my stories in Canada, I was assisted by the following: Ken Reddig of the Centre for Mennonite Brethren Studies in Canada; Lawrence Klippenstein of the Mennonite Heritage Centre; the staff of the library of the University of Winnipeg; and Christine Bell of Menno Simons College and Judi Hanson in the dean's office of the University of Winnipeg who typed the stories efficiently and cheerfully. My university deserves a special thanks for the half-year study leave in the fall of 1990, during which many of the stories were written.

My heartfelt gratitude goes to my colleague, Professor Al Reimer, who read the entire manuscript for style and offered valuable suggestions, many of which have been incorporated in the final version of the stories. Ever since I came to the University of Winnipeg in 1978, Al has been my close friend, co-worker and supporter.

I am also indebted to the many friends who were willing either to read or listen to my stories and offer their helpful criticism and suggestions. Among these readers and listeners, I wish to mention especially my brother and sister-in-law John and Beth Loewen of Kelowna, British Columbia, and my wife, Gertrude, who read or heard these stories many times over.

The credit for the format and appearance of this book goes to Paul M. Schrock, Michael A. King, and their staff at Herald Press and Mennonite Publishing House. To all, my thanks.

—Harry Loewen
Winnipeg, Manitoba

NO
PERMANENT
CITY

1

The Radical Disturber

On a Sunday morning, January 29, 1525, there was great commotion in the Zollikon church near Zürich, Switzerland. As the Reformed pastor, Nicolas Billeter, came in to preach, a tall young man rose from among the congregation. In clear and loud voice he asked, "What have you come to do?"

"I have come to preach the Word of God," the mild-mannered pastor replied.

"Not you but I," the young man shouted back, "have been called to preach the Word."

The pastor ignored the disturber, ascended the pulpit, and began to preach. The young man, however, continued rudely to talk back to the pastor. The pastor discontinued the service, stepped down from the pulpit, and headed for the door.

The congregation, siding with their pastor, insisted that he continue his sermon and that the disturber keep silent. When the pastor returned to the pulpit and resumed preaching, the troublemaker struck the pew with a stick, shouting, "It is written, my house shall be a house of prayer, but you have made it a den of thieves."

The radical young man had obviously gone too far. The deputy magistrate, who was present this Sunday morning, stepped forward. He commanded the young man to be quiet or face arrest and jail. The man sat down quietly and Pastor Billeter preached his sermon to the end.

The young man who disturbed the Reformed church service was George Blaurock, a radical Anabaptist. Of humble peasant background, Blaurock was a man of striking appearance. His black hair and beard and his fiery eyes betrayed an impulsive character. He had attended universities, but not for long. Having worked for some time as a village priest, he was a man of the common people, indifferent to theological and scholarly niceties. His name, which means "Bluejacket" in German, came from his habit of wearing a blue jacket.

George Blaurock belonged to a group of young people in the Zürich area who welcomed the Reformation and appreciated Ulrich Zwingli's sermons and courage. Together with Conrad Grebel, Felix Manz and others, he had supported Zwingli's fearless preaching against abuses and low moral standards within the old church. These young men believed with Zwingli, Martin Luther, and other reformers that giving the ordinary people the Word of God in their own language would foster much needed reform and renewal of faith and morals.

The young men around Zwingli, however, felt that the Reformers were too timid and slow. Believing the church needed to be restored to what it had been during the time of Christ and the apostles, the radical reformers, as the Anabaptists came to be known, sought to abolish the baptism of babies. They wanted to baptize only adults who had repented of their sinful life, professed Jesus as Redeemer and Lord, and were willing to follow him in their practical lives.

For the Anabaptists, following Jesus also included living in peace with all people, avoiding all violence, not participating in any war, and dealing justly in all areas of life. Particularly the common people, the peasants and workers, were to benefit from a thoroughgoing reformation of the religious, political, and economic institutions of that time. This is why the Anabaptists often sympathized and sided with the common people and against those who oppressed them.

Because of their radical views and beliefs, the Anabaptists were feared and hated by the established churches and governments. Even main reformers like Luther and Zwingli opposed the radicalism of the Anabaptists. Debates were held to discredit the Anabaptists' beliefs; the rulers began to enforce the old religious practices, including infant baptism and church attendance. The radicals were forbidden to preach and propagate their views and interpretation of the Bible. They were threatened with exile and even death if they refused to submit to the spiritual and governmental authorities and their regulations and laws.

After many efforts to bring about a thorough reformation of Swiss society, a group of some fifteen young men met in the house of Felix Mantz's mother in Zürich to discuss further plans and possible action. These radical reformers knew they would either have to submit to Zwingli and the city council or face punishment for not baptizing their infant children as had long been the custom.

During a time of Bible study, prayer, and discussion about what it meant to be a follower of Christ, George Blaurock rose. He asked Conrad Grebel, one of the acknowledged leaders of the group, to baptize him upon his confession of faith. As Blaurock knelt, Grebel took water in a dipper and poured it on his friend's head in the name of the triune God, thus performing the first adult baptism in the sixteenth century.

This was the beginning of the Anabaptist-Mennonite movement. The others who were present also requested to be baptized after declaring their faith and readiness to live as Christians in their society. George Blaurock administered the ordinance of baptism to each of them. This event took place on January 21, 1525.

After this momentous occasion, the group dispersed to preach the gospel and baptize other believers upon their declared faith. They proclaimed the Anabaptist message and baptized in public squares, near wells and rivers, in private homes, in open fields, and in caves and forests.

In the town of Zollikon, they were especially successful. Between January 22 and 29, they baptized about thirty-five men and women there. Little wonder that Blaurock believed the majority of the people of Zollikon would rather listen to him preach than to the Zwinglian pastor that Sunday morning. But in this he was badly mistaken. His zeal and impatience had clouded his judgment and good sense.

Yet "the new Paul," as Blaurock was called by his friends, was not discouraged by opposition or failure. After weeks of successful preaching, teaching, and baptizing among the small farmers of the Grüningen area in the late summer of 1525, Blaurock made another attempt to win an entire community for the Anabaptist cause. He went to the Reformed church at Hinwil on a Sunday morning before Pastor Johannes Brennwald had arrived.

Stepping behind the pulpit, Blaurock rhetorically asked whose pulpit this was. Then he said to the assembled congregation, "If it is God's place, where the Word of God should be proclaimed, then I am here as one sent by the heavenly Father to preach the Word of God."

John Allen Moore describes what followed. "After the intruder had been holding forth for a time, Pastor Johannes Brennwald came in. A mild-mannered and cautious man, he waited quietly and allowed Blaurock to continue. However, when the latter began to attack infant baptism, Brennwald felt it his duty to speak out and he did so.

" 'Do you defend infant baptism and propose to keep it?' asked Blaurock.

" 'Yes,' replied the pastor.

" 'Then you are anti-Christian and mislead the people,' cried Blaurock in the manner of a prophet. As the two men argued, the people became noisy, most of them supporting the Anabaptist."

With the help of other law enforcement officers, the deputy magistrate eventually arrested Blaurock and imprisoned him with other Anabaptists. However, Blaurock soon escaped and went to preach elsewhere.

In 1529 he was arrested in Austria. It was charged that "he had forsaken the priestly office, rejected infant baptism, taught a new baptism, would have nothing more to do with the mass, and did not believe that Christ was bodily in the wine and bread." Refusing to recant his "errors" and to betray the whereabouts of other Anabaptists, Blaurock was sentenced to death. On June 2, 1529, he was burned at the stake just outside of Innsbruck.

In the *Ausbund*, an Anabaptist collection of songs, two hymns are attributed to George Blaurock. In his "death hymn" "Forget Me Not, O Lord" Blaurock prays for himself and for those who persecuted him: "With all my heart I pray to you for all our enemies . . . that you, O Lord, lay not their misdeeds to their charge. And so I take my leave. May we remain in faith, undoubting, his holy work completing, and may he give us strength to face the end."

When the early Anabaptist leaders found that they were opposed on all sides, rejected by the great mass of people, and banished and sentenced to die by the spiritual and political authorities, they abandoned their attempts to reform entire communities and society. Instead they began to emphasize the renewal of individual persons, separation of their members from the world and what they considered worldly churches, and the establishment of Christian communities which were to model following Jesus. The Mennonites, Baptists, Brethren in Christ, Hutterites, Amish, and other "free churches" today trace their spiritual heritage back to these sixteenth-century Anabaptists.

2

The Doubting Priest

*T*he year 1524 was an important one for the village of Pingjum, in northern Holland, and for a twenty-eight-year-old man. That year Menno Simons was installed as a Catholic priest in his paternal village. Menno joined two other priests to serve in the church. One was the senior pastor, a well-educated man; the other, about Menno's age, was a priest slightly below Menno in rank.

According to Menno, both priests knew the Bible a little. But he himself "had never touched" Scriptures, for he feared if he read them he would be misled. Menno adds, "Behold, such an ignorant preacher was I for nearly two years."

Whatever Menno's opinion of himself, there is evidence that he was educated by the Premonstratensian Order, known as the first order to see education as an important aspect of its work. The Order's emphasis on simplicity and discipleship, renunciation of force in their mission programs, and peace were to become important parts of Menno's faith and life. Thus while Menno was not as learned as the other great Reformers, he knew Latin and Greek in addition to his native language of Dutch. In time he became acquainted with the writings of the church fathers and, of course, the Bible.

Menno's first theological doubts occurred when as a priest he administered the bread and wine during mass. Did the bread and wine really turn into the body and blood of Christ as the church taught? He thought at first that it was the devil who sought to lead him astray from his faith with these doubts. After confessing doubts to his father confessor, he still sighed and prayed about this but could find neither clarity nor peace.

In the meantime, the young priest Menno sought diversions in playing cards together with other priests in the village, drinking, and idling away precious time. When he touched on his doubts and what Scriptures might have to say about the divine mysteries such as the sacrament of the Last Supper, his companions ridiculed him. Menno could not even express his doubts and questions clearly, "so concealed was the Word of God from my eyes."

Finally Menno consulted the New Testament and began to read the Reformers, notably Martin Luther, Bucer, Bullinger, and others. While Luther convinced him that "human injunctions cannot bind unto eternal death," Menno found that the theologians varied greatly among themselves, "each following his own wisdom" and not the Word of God.

As Menno continued to study the Bible, his preaching improved to the extent that some in his congregation considered him to be "an evangelical preacher." As Menno writes, "Everyone sought and desired me; the world loved me and I loved the world. It was said that I preached the Word of God and was a good fellow."

While Menno served his congregation in Pingjum, an event helped to change his life. News reached him that in Leeuwarden a God-fearing man by the name of Sicke Freerks was beheaded for being rebaptized. It sounded strange to Menno to hear of a second baptism. Until then he had not known the Anabaptists, or brethren, as they called themselves, who rejected the baptism of infants and baptized only persons who confessed faith in Christ.

Again Menno examined the Bible, discussed infant and adult baptism with his pastor, and consulted the writings of the Reformers. He came to the conclusion "that there was no basis for infant baptism in Scripture." Even the church fathers, according to Menno, had no clear understanding concerning the meaning and practice of baptism. "Then I realized," Menno states, "that we were deceived in regard to infant baptism."

When Menno was transferred to Witmarsum in Friesland, the vil-

lage of his birth, he continued to serve the church to the best of his ability. But he knew that his preaching and service were "without spirituality or love," as he put it. In Witmarsum he also got to know the Anabaptists, both the peaceful kind and the violent Münsterites, who established their kingdom in the Westphalian capital in 1534.

Menno was much troubled by what happened in Münster and elsewhere where the followers of Jan Matthys and Jan van Leyden sought to establish themselves. "I did what I could to oppose them by preaching and exhortations, as much as in me was," he writes, "but my admonitions did not help, because I myself still did that which I knew was not right."

Another incident proved to be revolutionary in Menno's life. In March 1535, a group of radical Anabaptists, most likely followers of Melchior Hoffman, seized an old monastery near Bolsward by force. Then they were slaughtered by the authorities. Among the persons killed was Peter Simons, most likely Menno's brother. After this incident and a little later that year, when the Münster Anabaptists were defeated and cruelly killed by the combined forces of the Catholics and Protestant princes, Menno felt responsible for the tragedies.

"After this had transpired," he wrote, "the blood of these people, although misled, fell so hot on my heart that I could not stand it, nor find rest in my soul. . . . I saw that these zealous children, although in error, willingly gave their lives and their estates for their doctrine and faith. And I was one of those who had disclosed to some of them the abominations of the papal system. But I myself continued in my comfortable life and acknowledged abominations simply in order that I might enjoy physical comfort and escape the cross of Christ."

Thus in 1536 Menno began to publicly preach repentance and to point people to the narrow path of Christian discipleship. He also began to teach "the true baptism and the Lord's Supper, according to the doctrine of Christ." With that he cut himself off from the old church and became one of the Anabaptists, "the poor straying sheep who wandered as sheep without a proper shepherd."

Recognizing Menno's gifts, sincerity, and leadership ability, some seven or eight persons from the Anabaptist community approached the ex-priest and urged him "to put to good use the talents" which he had received. After much soul-searching and prayer, Menno agreed to become a leader of the Anabaptists and was ordained as an elder by the Dutch Anabaptist Obbe Philips. As Menno expressed it, "And so I, a miserable sinner, was enlightened of the Lord, was converted to a new mind, fled from Babel, entered into Jerusalem, and finally, though unworthy, was called to His high and heavy service."

And a heavy service it was. Constantly fleeing his persecutors, Menno preached, baptized, and wrote and published books. He tried to provide for his wife, Gertrude, and family, settled disputes among his followers, and was a leading Anabaptist figure and leader at numerous conferences. He thus became the acknowledged leader of that peaceful wing of Anabaptism which to this day bears the name "Mennonite."

Menno Simons died in 1561 near Bad Oldesloe, Germany. He was buried near the spot where today the "Menno Hut" and the "Menno Lindentree" stand. On a simple plaque are inscribed the words which became his lifelong motto and which he used as a preface for all his published works. "For no other foundation can anyone lay than that which is laid, which is Jesus Christ" (1 Cor. 3:11).

3

The Little Swan of Emden

*I*n Emden, East Friesland, Germany, there lived in the middle of the sixteenth century a woman named Swaen Rutgers and her husband. *Swaen* means "swan" and Swaen was sometimes called *Zwaantje*, which means "little swan" and may imply she was well liked by her neighbors and members of her congregation.

The Rutgers were members of the Mennonite congregation of which Leenard Bouwens was the elder. Bouwens was a zealous Mennonite preacher and evangelist. In some thirty years of ministry, he had preached many sermons and baptized well over 10,000 persons. He was thus, in terms of numbers of converts and baptisms, the most successful minister in that early period of Dutch-German Mennonitism. But one woman in his congregation opposed this powerful elder and contributed to a significant controversy. This woman was Swaen Rutgers.

The early Anabaptist-Mennonite church was very much concerned about its moral purity and that of individual members. All early leaders, including Menno Simons, Dirk Philips, and, of course, Leenard Bouwens, were strict about the faith and life of their members, although Menno was at first more lenient toward erring members than his fellow elders.

It is not known what Brother Rutger's failing was, but he was for some reason excommunicated and subsequently banned by Bou-

wens. According to the strict application of the ban, Rutgers was to
be avoided by members of his congregation in the hope that he
would repent of his sin and eventually come back to the church.
Not only was he to be shunned by his brothers and sisters, his wife
too was ordered to deny her husband "table and bed." This marital
avoidance, as it was called, was the ultimate punishment a trans-
gressor in the congregation could be given.

The question now was what Swaen Rutgers would do. Would she
comply with this harsh rule and thus alienate her husband, or
would she disobey and thus bring displeasure and possible excommunication by Bouwens on herself? Swaen decided to defy Bouwens and the church rule. She sided with her husband. In her distress she turned to her many friends in the Emden church and in
other places. She appealed to Menno Simons himself to help settle
the matter in her favor. Other members of the Emden church also
wrote Menno in support of Swaen.

Menno Simons now had to referee between the two disputing
factions. On the one hand, his heart went out to Swaen and her
case. On the other hand, he agreed with his fellow elders that sin
had to be dealt with and members who refused to repent of their
sinfulness had to be disciplined. However, he could not agree with
his strict fellow elders that marital avoidance did any good or was
supported by Scripture.

In November 1556, Menno wrote a letter to the church in Emden
concerning marital avoidance. He began by stating, "With great
sadness of heart I inform my dear brethren that I receive one com-
plaining letter after another, touching the relation of husband and
wife in regard to the ban; so that I notice great sadness with
many—a matter that does not surprise me at all; for from the beginning of my service, yes, more than twenty years, I have been dis-
tressed with great fear concerning this matter to this very hour, and
cannot bring myself to agree with the extremism which is in evidence in the Netherlands just now."

Menno agreed that adulterers, thieves, and apostates from the
faith had to be disciplined by the church. But if a church member
was a believer and had not committed any grave sins, then decided
not to avoid his or her mate, such a person should not be banned.
Husband and wife are one flesh and separating the two "is fraught
with much danger."

"In view of this," Menno added, "my heart was filled with much sorrow on hearing that a certain length of time was given Zwaantje Rutgers in which to leave her husband, or that in case of her failure to leave him, she was to be delivered up to Satan and excommunicated." Menno concluded, "Excommunication is instituted for reformation and not for destruction. Oh, that all were of one mind with me in this matter!"

Sadly, not all were of one mind with Menno. The Swaen Rutgers case did not end happily. As a result of the harsh application of the ban there were several divisions within the Dutch-North German Anabaptist community. The Swiss Anabaptists and those from southern Germany generally disagreed with the Dutch and North German churches' harsh position on the ban.

Menno Simons himself, at first more lenient with regard to the ban, was threatened with excommunication by the Leenard Bouwens' party. Bouwens, unyielding to the end, banned Swaen Rutgers. A year later, in 1557, at a meeting called to discuss marital avoidance, Menno Simons was won over to the strict practice of Leenard Bouwens and Dirk Philips.

But the story does not end there. Leenard Bouwens experienced hardships as well. After Menno Simons' death, he was accused by the church of domineering ambition, accepting money for spiritual services, and wine-drinking. As a result he remained inactive for several years, and in 1565 Dirk Philips deposed him along with six other fellow elders. There are no records to tell us what happened further to Swaen Rutgers and her husband, but we know that the issue of marital avoidance has plagued Mennonites until the present time.

4

The Tragedy of a Woman

*E*lizabeth Wantscherer was a young and beautiful Anabaptist woman. Unhappily married to Reiner von Hardrewijk, she left her husband. She sought to escape from Münster in Westphalia, where the revolutionary Anabaptists had set up their "kingdom" in 1534. Among the radical changes which the Anabaptist leaders introduced in the city, the holding of many wives was one of the worst as far as Elizabeth was concerned. She thought polygamy degrading to her sex and immoral.

When her husband discovered that Elizabeth was missing, a search party was formed. She was eventually found outside the city gates where she was hiding, returned to Münster, and was reconciled to her husband. When a few days later her husband died, she married Augustin Torrentius.

But she was not happy with her second husband either. She applied for divorce in the name of the "king" of Münster, Jan van Leyden. The basis of her request was that she had been forced by her strict father to marry her second husband.

Elizabeth's father, a member of the king's council, agreed he had compelled his daughter to marry Augustin Torrentius and the marriage was annulled. Her father, however, accused Elizabeth of superficial and easy living and of refusing to submit to her husband. It was about time, he argued, that women learned obedience to their husbands, for women everywhere were getting the upper hand and becoming too independent.

The religious leaders in the city basically agreed with Elizabeth's accuser. In fact, Bernard Rothman had argued in his writings that polygamy was one way of keeping women in check and bound to a husband whose duty it was to rule over her and thus keep order in the community. The example for this was the patriarchal time in the Bible, when godly men like Abraham and Jacob had several wives and concubines. Now, Rothman had argued, polygamy was another biblical practice in need of restoration.

Elizabeth Wantscherer, finding herself thus accused by her own father and feeling repulsion at the new practices in Münster, exclaimed, "I don't agree. I don't think that there is a man in this city who will tame me!"

On learning of the stubborn audacity of this rebellious young woman, King Jan van Leyden had Elizabeth thrown into prison. However, two days later he had her brought before himself, eager to see the woman who thus dared defy the laws of the city.

The king was struck with Elizabeth's beauty and noble figure. He said to her, "If you promise to behave yourself in the future and become an obedient woman, I will marry you."

Elizabeth, hoping to better her life, said to the king, "Majestic King, if your handmaiden has found favor in the king's eyes, I will not only obey you in all things, but I will also wash the feet of all the king's women and be willing to perform the most menial tasks in his household."

Elizabeth found grace in the king's eyes. She did not become a washerwoman or a maidservant of the king. She became his wife and for six months was called the Queen of King Jan van Leyden.

However, Elizabeth began to regret her decision when she saw the godlessness, the opulent and extravagant life of the king, his boundless sinful lust on the one hand—and on the other the suffering, complaints, and tears of people dying of hunger. She returned her rings and the other jewels Jan van Leyden, the King of Zion, as he was called, had given her. On her knees she asked him to allow her to leave the city.

The king's anger knew no bounds. He shouted, "At last your falseness, deceit and cunning, disobedience and rebellion come to the fore! I'll teach you and your kind a lesson!"

On May 12, 1534, Jan van Leyden dragged Elizabeth with his own hands to the marketplace. He decapitated her with his sword before all the people and his concubines, then he trampled her body with his feet.

After this inhuman execution, the other concubines of the king sang the hymn "To God on High Alone Be Honor!" Then the king and his court celebrated openly on the marketplace with dances, food, and drink.

The king excused his cruel deed by saying Elizabeth deserved death as a godless, sinful woman. "She was a whore," he exclaimed, "and one inclined toward disobedience and rebellion. That's why our heavenly Father commanded me to put her out of the way."

5

No Man Ever Touched Me

*E*lizabeth was destined to become a nun. Still a child, she had been taken by her parents to Tienge, a convent near Leer in East Friesland, Germany. At the age of twelve, she heard that a heretic had been burned to death because he did not believe in the sacraments of the church. This made a great impression on Elizabeth. Wishing to learn more about the sacraments and possible reasons for rejecting them, she acquired and began to read a Latin Bible. The more she read the more she doubted the doctrines of her church.

When Elizabeth became a young woman, she could not keep her doubts to herself. She talk with the other sisters about what troubled her. Suspected of heresy, Elizabeth was imprisoned in the convent for a year. When her fellow nuns pleaded with the prioress to set Elizabeth free, she was released from confinement but kept under constant supervision. Finding her condition unbearable, Elizabeth sought to escape from the convent. With the help of convent servants, she disguised herself as a milkmaid and left for the nearby town of Leer.

In Leer, Elizabeth was kindly received in the home of Mennonites, though she did not know her hosts belonged to that religious community. She attended the Mennonite worship services in Leer, was soon baptized, and joined the church as an active member. Fearing she might be detected and returned to the convent, Elizabeth moved to Leeuwarden. There she was taken into the house of a Mennonite woman named Hadewyck.

Hadewyck was the widow of a soldier who had been forced to be present when in 1531 his former friend Sicke Freerks was martyred for his faith. Hadewyck's husband had to beat the drum during the execution so the martyr could not address the people. The soldier angrily accused the authorities of inhumanity and cruelty and consequently had to flee to save his own life. Hadewyck had not heard from her husband since. She feared he had been secretly murdered. Hadewyck herself turned from the old church and became a Mennonite believer. There is reason to believe she was baptized by Menno Simons himself.

For a while the two women lived quietly and undisturbed, but within them was a strong desire to share their faith with others in their community. Putting caution aside, they began to take an active part in community life, serving the needs of fellow believers and proclaiming and teaching their faith to persons attracted to them.

Elizabeth especially had the gift of teaching. At her later trial, she was called a "teacheress" among the Anabaptists. That she was close to other Anabaptist elders and leaders, including Menno Simons, we learn from the fact that her accusers called her Menno's wife. It is possible that Elizabeth was often seen with Menno, who no doubt conferred with her in spiritual matters.

Soon both women were accused of spreading false teachings and put in prison. Hadewyck managed somehow to escape. Elizabeth, however, was brought before the judges in 1549 and tried for heresy. Her trial has been recorded in the *Martyrs Mirror* (compiled by Thieleman J. van Braght and first published in 1660).

At her trial Elizabeth was first asked to state upon oath whether she was married.

Elizabeth: "We are not permitted to swear. Our words ought to be simply 'yes' or 'no.' I have no husband."

Lords: "We know that you are a teacher who has led many persons astray. We demand to know who your friends are."

Elizabeth: "God has commanded me to love him and to honor my parents. I will not tell you who my parents or who my friends are, for that would mean their destruction."

Lords: "We shall leave you in peace about your friends, but tell us who the persons are whom you have taught."

Elizabeth: "O my lords, leave me in peace about my fellow believers, but ask me instead about my faith. I shall tell you gladly about it."

Lords: "We shall frighten you until you tell us whatever we wish to know."

Elizabeth: "Through God's help, I shall keep my tongue in check. I don't wish to become a traitor and thus deliver my brethren into your hands."

Lords: "Who were the persons present at your baptism?"

Elizabeth: "Christ said: 'Ask those persons who were there or who had heard about it.' "

Lords: "Now we know that your are a teacher, for you are identifying yourself with Christ himself."

Elizabeth: "No, my lords, I am a simple maid and servant in the house of God."

Lords: "What according to you is the house of God? Is our church not the house of God?"

Elizabeth: "No, my lords, for it is written that his followers are the temple of God and that he will dwell among them."

Lords: "What do you think of the sacrament of the mass?"

Elizabeth: "Nowhere in Scriptures have I read about a holy sacrament. But I have read about the Lord's Supper in the Bible."

Lords: "You are an impudent and arrogant woman."

Elizabeth: "No, my lords, I merely speak to you freely and according to my understanding of God's Word."

Lords: "What do you think of infant baptism? You were baptized again, were you not?"

Elizabeth: "No, my lords, I was not baptized again. I have been baptized only once upon my confession of faith in Christ and according to Scriptures."

Lords: "Do you think that our children are damned because they were baptized?"

Elizabeth: "No, my lords, far be it from me to judge little children."

Lords: "Don't you think there is salvation in baptism?"

Elizabeth: "No, my lords, all the oceans of the world cannot save me. It is Christ who redeems us according to his commandment: Love God above all else and your neighbor as yourself."

Lords: "Don't you think priests have the power to forgive sins?"

Elizabeth: "No, my lords, how can I believe that? I say that Christ is the only priest who can forgive sins."

Lords: "Are you not in need of forgiveness? Have you not denied the necessity of confession and the sacraments?"

Elizabeth: "I confess that I have transgressed the decrees and commands of the pope and the emperor. But show me on the basis of the Scriptures that I have transgressed the commandments of my Lord and God. If I have done so, I shall admit that I am a miserable sinner and in need of forgiveness."

Lords: "Enough of this! We have tried to bring you back to your faith with all patience and love. But you are stubborn and arrogant. We shall now try to persuade you with severity."

"Master Hans, seize her!" the Procurator General said to his henchman nearby.

Elizabeth was taken to the torture chamber. The executioner applied the thumbscrews to her thumbs and forefingers until blood squirted out at the nails. Enduring the great pain, Elizabeth prayed, "Help me, O Lord, your poor handmaiden!"

When they applied the screws to her shins, one on each, Elizabeth pleaded, "O my lords, do not put me to shame, for no man ever touched my bare body."

When her tormentors saw she would not recant nor return to the old faith, Elizabeth was condemned to die by drowning. Sentence was passed on Elizabeth Dirks on March 27, 1549. Thus she offered her body to God.

Many Anabaptists in the sixteenth and seventeenth centuries yielded under pressure and returned to the old church. But there were also many men and women who like Elizabeth Dirks were tortured and executed because they followed the dictates of their conscience and wished to be free in matters of religious faith. In the Netherlands and in northern Germany alone, some 2000 persons were martyred to death, more than one third of them women.

In letters and public testimonies, these men and women expressed their fear of torture and death. But they also admonished their loved ones and others to follow their faith and to remain courageous and strong when compelled to pay the supreme price for what they believed.

6

No Permanent City

*I*n the Emmenthal Valley of Switzerland lies the village of Eggiwil, which until the beginning of the eighteenth century belonged to the parish of Würzbrunnen. High above the valley, about a quarter of an hour walking distance from Eggiwil, stands an old gray farmhouse. Above the entrance of the house, the visitor can see the date 1648 carved into wood. On either side of the date, the initials J.B. and A.S. are visible. These letters tell us Jacob Brönnimann and Anna Steiner built this house in 1648.

The Brönnimanns were well-to-do and respected farmers in the area. Lush meadows and carefully tilled acres of land surrounded their neatly kept farm buildings. As far as their neighbors were concerned, only one thing was wrong with the builders of the house and their descendants—they were suspected of being Anabaptists or at least sympathizers of this hated sect.

The authorities kept a watchful eye on the Brönnimanns. A brother of Jacob had left the area in 1671 because of his Anabaptist faith and settled in the Palatinate. His possessions had been confiscated by the spiteful and greedy "gracious lords." The same would happen to the Brönnimanns if only the authorities could find a legitimate reason to move against them.

When Jacob died, his son Hans also managed to keep his Anabaptist faith secret. Gossip had it that Hans attended Anabaptist worship services, but no one could prove anything. When the Reformed pastor of Würzbrunnen was asked about this, he answered, "Hans Brönnimann may be a secret Anabaptist, and if he is one, which I don't know, I wish that all Emmenthalers were people like he is."

Abraham Brönnimann, the son of Hans and grandson of the builder of the house, was a tall man, strong and respected by all in his community. He married Magdalena Engel, a known Anabaptist of Rötenbach. Magdalena attended Anabaptist services regularly and openly and her husband did not object.

Magdalena died just before severe persecutions of Anabaptists broke out again, leaving behind her husband and Anna, their two-year-old daughter. Abraham, who never married again, kept his faith hidden from the authorities. But many of his friends and relatives in the valley were affected by the severe decrees against the Anabaptists. Abraham helped these unfortunate people as well as he could, hiding some of them in his house and aiding others with advice and material means.

As the years passed, the Anabaptists who remained in the valley adjusted to the situation around them. They often held their meetings at night and in such hidden places as forests and mountain areas. In the meantime Anna, Abraham's daughter, had become a young woman resembling her deceased mother. Her father would have liked to see her married to Jacob Stetler, a son of his neighbor, but Anna had other plans. She loved Johannes Steiner of Rötenbach and had promised to marry him. Abraham eventually agreed, for Johannes was a fine young man and a descendant of Abraham's grandmother, Anna Steiner.

Before long Johannes Steiner went to the pastor in Würzbrunnen to make arrangements for his marriage with Anna. When he told the pastor that he wished to get married, the elderly clergyman asked, "Well, well, and who, if I may ask, is the chosen bride?"

Blushing slightly, Johannes said, "It is Anna Brönnimann of Eggiwil."

The pastor smiled and commented, "Well, you're marrying into a good and well-to-do family." After a slight pause, the pastor continued, "I have one question. Does Anna belong to the Anabaptists as her mother did, and is her father also a member of their congregation?"

"To be honest with you, Pastor," Johannes replied, "I've never asked about this. As you know yourself, Anna's mother was an Anabaptist, and her relatives, also Anabaptists, were driven from the area when Anna was about two years old. Whether Anna's father is an Anabaptist I don't know, but one thing I do know—he's a quiet, good and God-fearing man. It's my desire to become a Christian like him."

After this animated speech, Johannes paused briefly, then said more quietly, "At the moment Anna's father is not too well. He hopes that our wedding can take place soon so that arrangements for the future of his daughter and the farm can be made."

"Don't misunderstand me," said the pastor warmly. "I respect the Anabaptists very much. They're right in many ways and our people would do well to live their Christian lives as they do. I must tell you, however, in my position as pastor, I'm obligated to ask questions about whether people are Anabaptists or not. You should know, though, that it's difficult for me to do so."

Johannes accepted the pastor's explanation. Then the pastor asked, "Tell me, young man, why do you want me to marry you? You could ask someone else."

"You have married my parents and Anna's parents," Johannes said, "and thus Anna and I wish to be married by you."

After making arrangements for the wedding, Johannes left for home, telling Anna and her father what the pastor had told him.

"It's true," Abraham said, "the pastor and the enemies of the Anabaptists never knew whether we had formally joined the congregation. My grandfather and father as well as my grandmother and mother were members of the fellowship.

"However, for fear of suffering and losing all we had, we never held meetings in our house. And since we seldom came among people and did not associate publicly with Anabaptists, the fact that we were and are Anabaptists remained a secret to our neighbors."

Abraham fell silent and bowed his head. "Our friends and relatives, the Eichenbergers, the Krähenbühls, the Stetlers, the Steiners, and the Engels paid dearly for professing the Anabaptist faith openly. They were banished and the authorities confiscated their property. It wasn't right to be so attached to our material things. If our people are persecuted again, I'll join the congregation formally at once.

"Last night Peter, a nephew of mine and a cousin of Anna's, came here from the distant Palatinate. He came to claim his inheritance in Kurzenberg. He said that he and his people are doing well in the Palatinate. They have rented land, they have lovely farms surrounded by forests, and there are even mountains there—but, of course, they're not our Swiss mountains!"

Becoming more serious, Abraham continued, "I must tell you something else. Last night, after Peter was asleep, I heard a strange noise outside. When I tiptoed to the window, I saw a disguised figure hiding behind our pile of wood. It was no doubt a spy sent by the authorities to check on us. We must remain vigilant and, if necessary, prepared to leave all behind and move elsewhere."

"As long as the pastor of Würzbrunnen is on our side, nothing will happen to us," Johannes said confidently.

"Let's hope so," said his father, "but when it comes to the orders of our gracious lords, not even the pastor can help us much. I hope nothing will happen in the next few days, until you two are safely married."

Abraham Brönnimann's health remained stable, so he was able to accompany Anna and Johannes to Würzbrunnen, where they were married. After the ceremony Abraham said to the clergyman, "Next time you will come to me. My time on earth is up. I can feel it in my bones. I'm glad to see my daughter happy and well taken care of. And if bad times should come for the young couple, as happened to many of their relatives in the past, they will no doubt find a place somewhere where they can live according to their faith in peace."

"But my dear Brönnimann," the pastor exclaimed, "we don't die that soon. You're still younger than I am. I came as a young man to Würzbrunnen many years ago. I have buried your father and mother. I have married you and Helena, and I stood by you when your dear wife died. Now I have the joy of pronouncing the blessing upon your children's future course."

Turning serious and speaking more quietly, the pastor continued, "I have seen how the Anabaptists in this area were disowned and driven from their homes and land, and I have wept over the injustice done to these people. But I tell you, the time will come when we will recognize the mistakes we made. Those who were forced to leave their homeland were among the best that our fatherland had.

"I too will soon have to leave this world. It gives me comfort to know that I have never taken part in actions against these poor people. I've never informed the authorities against them."

Before the two men parted, the pastor said, "By the way, a few days ago a son of Lisbeth Engel was here to obtain certificates of his mother's baptism and marriage. He needed them for the purpose of getting the inheritance that had fallen to him. I provided him with the documents and also wrote a letter to the authorities not to cause the young man any difficulties."

"I'm very glad to hear that," Brönnimann said and shook the pastor's hand. "And now, dear pastor, may God be with you. We have to go home now."

The two men were not to see each other again. Before long Abraham fell seriously ill and died soon thereafter. The pastor of Würzbrunnen buried him as he had done Abraham's parents and wife. The pastor too followed the quiet Anabaptist shortly. Many had loved the good clergyman, including the Anabaptists. He was considered a friend of the persecuted people.

The years passed. Johannes and Anna lived in love and harmony, worked hard, and saved some money for a rainy day. Five children were born to the couple. Johannes and Anna joined the Anabaptist fellowship and became active members in the congregation. Johannes was chosen by the congregation to become a teacher-minister, a position the young man accepted as from the Lord. In his position Johannes traveled widely to instruct and comfort the scattered brothers and sisters. Anna often worried about her husband's fearless activity and strenuous work.

One day a friend brought the disheartening news that in Signau there was well-founded talk that harsh measures would again be taken against the Anabaptists. Johannes and Anna knew that the days in their beloved homeland were coming to an end. They soon made arrangements to sell their farm. A good buyer was found. The Steiners at least knew that their property would not pass into the hands of the grasping authorities.

Loading a wagon with the most necessary things, the Steiner family left their home quietly in the dead of night. They traveled past Solothurn and Basel until they came to friends and relatives in the

Alsace. But they could not stay there, so they continued north to the Palatinate where other Anabaptists, including some of their relatives, had earlier found refuge and a home.

Peter, Anna's cousin who had gone to Switzerland to claim his inheritance, took the Steiners into his home in Enkenbach. But eventually the Steiners would have to find a more permanent settlement, which was becoming more difficult. The thought of moving to America came up time and again, however much Anna dreaded the idea of spending some four months crossing the Atlantic and making a new beginning so far away.

When the Elector of the Palatinate began to discriminate against the Anabaptists, especially in matters of land acquisition and rental, the way for the Steiners became more clear. They would have to pack up and leave again. First they tried their fortune with Anabaptists in Holland. Traveling to Bingen by wagon, they embarked upon a ship called Hope, which took them along the Rhine River to Grüningen. There they purchased a piece of land, began to farm, and established themselves in the local congregation.

Three additional children were born to the Steiners and their material prosperity increased as well. But Johannes' heart was filled with sadness, which increased with time.

One day Anna said to him, "Johannes, what is it that worries you? We're well-off and we can live here in peace and security. Why aren't you happy?"

"It's not material things that worry me," said Johannes. "It's the conditions in the congregations here that give me concern. Members quarrel among themselves, they're suspicious of each other, and even among the servants of the Word, there is little genuine love.

"In our congregation parties are forming, divisions are taking place, and each side is pressuring one to join them. I've told them that I will not take sides and would rather move to America than stay where there's so much discord and a lack of love."

"I've always resisted the thought of moving to America," Anna said, "but perhaps the time has now come to leave the old world behind and begin a new life in the land of freedom."

They soon sold their farm and, together with other Mennonites, they traveled to Rotterdam where they boarded a ship bound for America. After a long journey across the sea, they at last set foot near Philadelphia. Relatives and friends welcomed the Steiner family warmly. Before long the Steiners acquired land, built a house, and began a new life in Pennsylvania.

The children of the Steiners grew up and became responsible young men and women. Abraham, the oldest son, fell in love with Elizabeth Brönnimann, a distant relative of the Steiners. Father Steiner had the joy of officiating at his children's wedding.

Mother Steiner said to her daughter-in-law, "I never thought, when we were still in Enkenbach, that you and my son would ever become a couple. How wonderful are God's ways! He has done all things well. We can say with the psalmist: 'The bird has found a resting place.' We too now have a home on earth, but the best thing is that we know of a permanent home above."

7

Exiles

*N*ight had descended on Langnau, a village in the Emmenthal Valley near Berne, Switzerland. A lonely man, Uli Steiner, was on his way to nearby Mättenberg. His wife had left him that evening; now he followed her in the hope that she would return home with him. He felt, however, that she was like a vanishing shadow, and he might lose her forever.

From some distance Uli saw her enter the house of the shoemaker, Michel Burkhalter. Other dark figures emerged, then disappeared quickly into the house. Coming closer Uli heard men and women singing in quiet tones.

As he listened he heard, "Dear Jesus Christ, our Lord, help us in our distress. . . . The last hour has come upon us. . . . We are hated, persecuted and exiled. . . . There is no place for us on earth. . . ."

The singing ended, and Uli Steiner heard someone pray fervently and loudly. In the flickering light of an oil lamp, he could make out toward the back of the room a row of kneeling figures. After the prayer they rose, sat on benches, and listened to the words of Michel Burkhalter.

Burkhalter first spoke of a new mandate which had been issued on April 6, 1693, according to which persons aged fourteen and over must appear before the magistrates and swear an oath of allegiance. Those unwilling to swear would be declared Anabaptists. Moreover, Anabaptist leaders should be apprehended and handed

over to the authorities. For the capture of a local leader a reward of twenty-five talers was offered and for the capture of one from another canton, fifty talers. Anabaptists who refused to take an oath would have until April 17 to leave the country.

Burkhalter then spoke of what it meant to be a Christian. Christian faith, he declared, comes from God as a gracious gift. It is received freely and voluntarily with no outside pressure or compulsion. To believe in Christ means to follow him in life, to do good to all people, to take on oneself the cross of suffering and persecution.

Burkhalter then reminded the group that Anabaptist leaders like Felix Mantz, Konrad Winkler, Hans Herzog, George Blaurock, and others were drowned, burned, and decapitated because of their faith. But this was the way, he continued. This was how the bride of Christ was being prepared for the marriage feast of the Lamb of God.

"So we too," he concluded, "are ready to pull up stakes and leave our homes. God himself will show us the way. In this life there is nothing but sorrow, distress, fear, and suffering. Blessed the person who can die with him and pray, 'Into your hands I commend my spirit, Lord.' Amen."

The prayer that followed made a deep impression on Uli Steiner. The shoemaker prayed, "Lord, have mercy upon us sinners. If there is something in us that displeases you, disclose it to us that we may repent of it and find your forgiveness. Be also merciful, dear Lord, to those who hate you and us, who persecute your followers. Forgive them their sins, for they don't know what they do. On account of us, do not hold their sins against them."

When the preacher fell silent, Uli saw the women inside the house weep and embrace and kiss one another. The men looked seriously and with determination at each other. Uli too felt a tear roll down his cheek. He slowly turned and headed for home. Now he knew he had lost his wife.

On April 17, 1693, a train of men, women, and children moved slowly along the way from Langnau north. They carried baskets and chests filled with their few earthly possessions. A few wept as they cast backward glances, some looked ahead with a serious determination, and a few walked as in a trance, smiling as they contemplated their reason for leaving home.

In the cool shade of a forest the homeless wanderers halted, put their burdens down and rested. From here they were able to see for the last time the hills and mountains of their beloved homeland. Someone began to sing a song attributed to George Blaurock. The last stanzas included the following lines. "I cannot rely upon the flesh, for it is weak and sinful. . . . I will build upon your Word, Lord, for it is my staff and shield. . . . With all my heart I plead with you, forgive all my sins, and also, dearest Lord, forgive the sins of all our enemies."

At a respectful distance stood a group of people, including Uli Steiner, who had hidden behind a bush. They saw how the Anabaptists took up their bundles again and started on their way northward. Uli had seen his wife for the last time.

The citizens of Langnau talked about the exile of the Anabaptists for a long time. The Emmenthalers were not given to a great display of emotion, but in quiet conversations they expressed their views about the government's mandate and the fate of their fellow citizens. Some applauded the action of the authorities. Some said it served them right, for they were the scum of Swiss society. Some felt sorry for what they called victims of false teachings and fanaticism.

Most Emmenthalers, however, felt a quiet anger about the actions of the magistrates and sympathy for the exiles. They felt that the exiles were of their own flesh and blood—and that the government, the pastors, the governor, and the "my lords" were not of their flesh and blood.

The Swiss-Anabaptist exiles usually found their way to Alsace, the Palatinate, regions along the Rhine River, the Netherlands, and North America.

8

An Ugly Affair

*F*or the Sobotiste Hutterite community and its bishop Andreas Ehrenpreis (1589-1662), 1633 was a difficult year. As the *Chronicle of the Hutterian Brethren* states, "That same year a very ugly affair was started" by a lord of Branc. The Hutterites were drawn into circumstances that threatened to undermine their long-standing principle of nonresistance. The sequence of events is instructive both to Hutterites and Mennonites who take their principles and heritage seriously.

Sobotiste was a town in Slovakia, Hungary, near the Moravian border. It had become the site of a large Hutterite Bruderhof (colony). In the sixteenth century, this market village belonged to the manorial nobleman Franz Niáry of Bedek, lord of the castle of Branc. Since the Lord of Branc needed good farmers and tenders of vineyards, in 1546 he invited the Hutterites from nearby Moravia to settle on his estate. When in 1622, during the Thirty Years' War, the Hutterites were expelled from Moravia altogether, many of them joined their coreligionists in Sobotiste.

The relationship between the Hutterites and their manorial lords was regulated periodically by terms set down in charters of privilege (*Hausbrief*) issued by the lords. One such charter was drawn up in 1613. It stipulated that the Hutterites were free to exercise their religion in exchange for an annual payment of money. Beyond this sum no additional obligations were to be placed on the community. The agreement between the two groups worked well until an incident on December 18, 1632, sparked a controversy between a lord of Branc and the brothers of Sobotiste.

On that December day Lord Franz Nagy-Michaly appeared at the Hutterite community. He demanded that the brothers harness six horses and take him across the mountains to Ziffer, a market town and castle some considerable distance away.

They could not oblige him, the Hutterites replied. He, Lord Franz, was not the only lord of Branc, and their additional service would set a bad precedent. The other lords, Ludwig and Bernhard Niáry and Caspar Tardy, co-owners of the Branc estates, might in the future demand similar services—contrary to the contract and privileges given the Hutterites by the lords' predecessors.

The refusal to serve him made Lord Franz very angry. He ordered his hussars and foresters to take the Hutterites' horses from the stable by force. In doing so, the hussars struck several brothers who were in the yard. "At this," the *Chronicle* states, "our people came running from all sides with flails, forks, sticks, and hoes to stop them, but our people did not attack them. The lord with his hussars rode away in a passion."

A few hours later Lord Franz sent his men to take the community's pigs from the field. The swineherds ran home shouting and reporting what was happening. According to the *Chronicle*, "several brothers gave chase, along with neighbors and some servants of Lord Ludwig Niáry, and got the pigs back. The raiders fled, wounded and bleeding. This enraged Lord Franz Nagy-Michaly even more, and he swore to take revenge."

Brother Heinrich Hartmann, a Hutterite servant of the Word, was sick at the time of the fracas. When he got well, he wrote an account of the whole affair and sent it to all the lords of Branc. The lords of the Niáry and Tardy families reassured the Hutterites that they had done nothing wrong in protecting their property in the face of injustice and violence.

Lord Franz, however, thought otherwise. He eventually persuaded the other lords to side with him against the Hutterites. A court was set up to try the Hutterites, with twelve noblemen acting as jurors. Brother Heinrich and several other brothers were summoned to appear in court on charges of insubordination to their manorial lord and wounding his men. The Hutterites refused to appear in court because, according to contract, they were not required to become entangled in civic affairs. They felt that if someone had just cause against them, the matter could be settled outside of court.

The Hutterites' case carried little weight with the authorities. Brother Heinrich and four other brothers were forced to appear in court. The prosecutor read the charges against them in Latin, describing how the Hutterites had run at their lord with pitchforks, flails, hoes, sticks, and other implements, with the intent to kill him. After the jurors had translated the indictment for the brothers, they demanded that Brother Heinrich give an answer to the charges.

With due humility and respect Brother Heinrich began, "My dear nobles of the jury and other lords present, you all know well how my brothers and I have respectfully asked to be exempt from going to court, since we are not instructed in the legal practices of the world or in Hungarian law, and it is against our conscience to go to court with our manorial lord."

He then explained that they had been compelled to appear in court to answer the charges against them. "I ask humbly," he continued, "that if I say something that is not quite correct according to law, that this is not held against me, as I have never learned the art of rhetoric."

When he was told to speak freely, Brother Heinrich said, "Dear lords, we have several manorial lords in Branc, and each one wants to have sole authority. Thus, instead of doing compulsory labor for so many lords, we made a contract to pay a fixed yearly sum in addition to the rent for our houses.

"Now, however, contrary to this agreement, we have been ordered to do compulsory labor by Lord Franz who even tried by force to take our horses from the stables and our pigs from the field. He himself caused the uproar because of the blows he dealt our people. So along with my brothers here, I have no guilt in that uproar.

"Moreover, we have seriously disciplined those of our people who were involved. If what happened has upset our lord, I humbly ask for pardon on my own behalf as well as that of my brothers."

The noble jurors retired to consult with one another. When they came back after some time, the brothers were told that according to

Hungarian law the parties should seek a settlement before judgment was passed. The Hutterites consulted with their people and with the Niáry lords as to what might be a reasonable settlement. These parties agreed that "for the sake of peace" Lord Franz might be offered a sum of forty imperial talers. All, including the jurors, felt this was a fair offer. Lord Franz, however, refused the offer.

Since no peace settlement could be reached, the prosecutor read the sentence: "According to present impartial judgment, it is understood that the brothers wanted, in their community, to strike their manorial lord dead, and therefore it is decided that all of them—men, women and children—are liable to the death penalty. However, the court will show them mercy by having only twelve leading brothers beheaded or taking a fine of forty gulden from each male person over twelve years of age."

The Hutterite community was devastated and feared worse things to come. In addition to this unjust sentence based on a falsehood, they also expected to be punished for wounding the lord's hussars when they tried to steal the pigs. Fortunately, however, the jurors ruled that the hussars got what they deserved. "Violence may be met with violence," they said, "but no subject has the right to rebel against his manorial lord."

Lord Franz and the Tardy lords were pleased that the court's judgment turned out in their favor. The next day they sent their men to record all male persons over twelve years of age and calculated forty gulden for each one, which amounted to a large sum. But the Hutterites refused to pay the lords anything, knowing they had been treated unjustly. Within their community they "pleaded in prayer that God through his grace might deliver them from their plight," as the *Chronicle* puts it.

In the meantime Brother Heinrich and his fellow brothers were forced to suffer in damp and cold prison cells. From time to time Lord Franz would come with fellow lords to check on the prisoners and to mock and threaten them. To his friends Lord Franz would say, "I have captured the king of the Anabaptists and his councilors who had tried to kill me."

At one point Lord Franz threatened to put the Hutterites in chains and force them to do heavy labor while in chains. He also threatened to flog them and sell them to a Hungarian captain at a border fortress. All this he did to intimidate the Hutterites, hoping that they would pay the ransom money for the prisoners.

Meanwhile the Niáry lords and their friends sought to secure the brothers' release from prison, trying everything in their power to change Lord Franz's mind. Eventually, after various efforts on the part of the Niáry lords and those of the Hutterites themselves, the prince of the region ordered Burgrave Stefan Palffy, chief of the district, to settle the matter. The wife of the burgrave also interceded on behalf of the brothers, making pleas and writing letters to other ladies and lords who might have some influence. As the *Chronicle* puts it, she left "no stone unturned in an effort to reach a settlement."

Feeling the pressure from all sides, Lord Franz came up with a face-saving device. He asserted that his court costs and the costs for the care of his wounded hussars had been high and that a money payment would be most welcome. The Hutterites offered an amount and Lord Franz accepted. The ugly affair ended on October 8, 1633.

The *Chronicle* concludes, "So the brothers returned to the church with unblemished consciences, and in great joy all the faithful praised and thanked God. One can see in all this what great problems there are when a subject incurs even the smallest guilt toward his manorial lord . . . even if many high ranking, honorable people acknowledge our innocence and testify to it. In the end, the Lord Franz Nagy-Michaly and his supporters earned more shame and dishonor than praise and profit."

The Hutterites' innocence had been vindicated before the law and the world. But in their own community they knew their self-defense and resort to armed resistance had been contrary to their traditional beliefs and practices. In an attempt to restore their members to Christian nonresistance, the elders, including Bishop Andreas Ehrenpreis, issued a letter of admonishment addressed to their communities.

The letter, dated November 28, 1633, pointed out that through their resistance the brothers had sinned not only against their conscience but against the Word of God which teaches Christians to submit to the governments above them. "To suffer damage or loss of worldly goods," the letter stated, "is better than to lose one's good conscience."

If in the future brothers become guilty under the law, the elders warned, the community would—on the basis of God's Word and in accordance with the tradition of its forebears—discipline and ban such persons. It would also allow them to suffer the punishment the worldly laws imposed.

The letter stressed the traditional "staff-bearing" of the Hutterites as opposed to the "sword-bearing" of those early Anabaptists who allowed their members to defend themselves or serve as soldiers in some instances. In going on a journey, or when tending pigs or cattle, a staff was sufficient, the letter stated. "Hooks" or other carnal weapons were not only contrary to the teaching of the gospel and Hutterite tradition, but also dangerous to the bearer of such weapons. They became a challenge to evil people who sought cause to hurt the followers of Jesus.

According to the letter, even wishing one's enemy's destruction or death was not worthy of Christ's disciples. "Do not curse the king in your heart nor the rich man in your closet," the elders warned, "for the birds of the air will surely make your secret thoughts public." Members of the community ought to live consistent Christian lives both in thought and in action, for "the field has eyes to see and the woods have ears to hear."

In conclusion the elders hoped that members of the community would fear God and conduct themselves according to Holy Scriptures. The elders asked those who had sinned to take off the stained cloaks of sin and put on garments of innocence washed in the blood of the Lamb. Striving after godliness would ensure individual salvation and the community's prosperity.

9

Dreamer
and Visionary

*T*oward the end of the seventeenth century, there appeared a man and a woman of advanced age on the streets of Germantown, a newly established settlement in Pennsylvania. The man tapped a white cane before him. The woman at his side held on to his arm, leading him toward the town hall. The old couple was poorly dressed, and the small bundles they carried contained all their possessions. Some curious children and adults followed the couple from a distance. Arriving at the town hall, the woman indicated to the man that they had arrived. They mounted the two or three steps and disappeared behind the door.

The Germantown court records for November 25, 1694, state that the Mennonites William Rittenhouse and Jan Doeden were to take a freewill collection. Its purpose was to provide the Plockhoys couple with a little house with trees and a garden at the "end street of the town." The small house was then built on a half-acre lot and donated to the Plockhoys. There they lived the rest of their lives. We know nothing about their last years, except that they were cared for by their fellow Mennonites.

Who were the Plockhoys and why had they come to this first German-Mennonite settlement in North America? What we know about Plockhoy is both interesting and significant.

Pieter Cornelisz Plockhoy was born in the city of Zierkzee in Zeeland (the Netherlands) of Mennonite parents. As a young man he went to Amsterdam where a friend of his, Galenus Abrahamsz de Haan, was a noted physician and minister of the Mennonite church. Both men believed that the gospel was to be freely accepted and practiced. There should be no compulsion whatever in matters of faith. Narrow views and religious fanaticism were far from the minds of the two men.

Because of their liberal views and beliefs, Plockhoy and de Haan were attracted to a group of people in Amsterdam known as Collegiants. Among the Collegiants were persons of Catholic and Protestant backgrounds. They met in halls and houses to discuss faith issues and sought to apply Christian principles to practical living. They believed church and state should be kept separate, that there should be no set and rigid creed in their fellowship, and that worship and preaching should be as informal as possible. The Collegiants baptized by immersion, administered the Lord's Supper among themselves, and stressed religious tolerance and acceptance of each others' individuality.

Within the community of the Collegiants Plockhoy was influenced toward the role he was later to play in England and America. Hoping to establish a community along the principles he learned among the Collegiants, Plockhoy set out for England in 1658. With the tolerant-minded Oliver Cromwell in power at this time, Plockhoy was confident that the Lord Protector would help him in his venture.

Plockhoy appeared before the governing council and was granted a personal interview with Cromwell, petitioning the Lord Protector to assist him in establishing a "little commonwealth." In it people of all religious backgrounds would be invited to work together and live by principles of justice, freedom, and community, "all for one and one for all."

We do not know how Cromwell reacted to Plockhoy's ideas, for he died shortly thereafter. In the turbulence which followed Cromwell's death and the restoration of the monarchy in England, the reform scheme of the Mennonite visionary was not realized.

Plockhoy outlined his ideas in several pamphlets written in 1659. The titles of these writings indicate what this social reformer had in mind. One pamphlet was called "The Way to Peace and Settlement." Another bore the title "A Way Proposed to Make the Poor . . . Happy."

In these writings Plockhoy stated that he intended to bring "together a fit, suitable, and well-qualified people into one household-government, or little commonwealth." In this community everyone would keep his own property "and be employed . . . without being oppressed." Plockhoy further stated that in this new community there would be no place for idle, evil, and disorderly persons. People who "live upon the labor of others" would not be tolerated.

The proposed community was to be composed of four classes of people—artisans, farmers, sailors, and masters of arts and science. The people in this community would work six hours each day with a day of rest on Sundays. Plockhoy envisioned a prosperous trade with the outside world which would benefit the entire community. Products would be sold at the lowest possible price. The people would live communally, eat together, and the profit of their work would go back to the society and be used for the good of all.

Encountering difficulties in England, Plockhoy in 1661 went back to Holland, where he began to promote the idea of a colony in North America. With twenty-four other Mennonite families Plockhoy approached the city of Amsterdam, requesting a tract of land in

New Netherlands, North America, and financial assistance to begin a settlement there. The burgomaster of Amsterdam approved the petition and on June 6, 1662, the contract was signed.

Plockhoy tried to encourage other potential emigrants to sail for New Netherlands. He invited the poor who did not know how to obtain a living in Holland and the affluent looking for peace of mind in the New World.

To interest settlers in going to America, Plockhoy worked out "117 Articles of Government." In the articles he stated that in the new community there would be exemption from military service, that the colony would be governed by its members, and that laws would be enacted by a majority of the legislators. A striking provision was the article stating that "no lordship or servile slavery" would burden the colony. This article was to become the first law to prohibit slavery in America.

At last on May 5, 1663, Plockhoy and some twenty-five Mennonite families sailed from Rotterdam on the ship *St. Jacob* for New Amstel where they arrived on July 28. Along the Delaware River, in the so-called "Valley of the Swans," they established their little commonwealth.

However, only one year later the English fleet attacked Manhattan, and the soldiers destroyed the forts and colonies along the Delaware River, including Plockhoy's settlement. According to some reports, the settlers were sold as slaves in Virginia. Some no doubt found their way back to Holland.

Plockhoy and his wife were granted in 1682 two lots in the new English town of Lewes in Delaware, on condition that they build a house on each lot or lose the land. Being old and nearly blind, Plockhoy was unable to fulfill his obligations. Ten years later the Plockhoys appeared in Germantown, where they were kindly received and cared for by fellow Mennonites.

Plockhoy was an idealist and dreamer. Taking the gospel seriously, he sought to practice what Jesus had taught his followers. As Plockhoy wrote, "For which end, that we may transmit the world into our posterity in a better condition than we first found it, I have contributed this little."

While Plockhoy's contribution to society may have been little, he certainly belongs to those of whom we read on the title page of one of his pamphlets: "Blessed is he who considers the poor" (Ps. 41:1).

10

A Teacher
with a Heart

One day Christopher Dock, the "pious schoolmaster of the Skippack," did not return home from school. Neighbors knew that normally the teacher stayed at school for some time after dismissing his pupils. He usually worked on some assignment or lesson for the next day, and he always prayed for each of his pupils in turn. When the neighbors went to look for him on this autumn day in 1771, they found him in the schoolroom on his knees—dead.

We do not know much about this pious teacher. He was born somewhere in the Palatinate, Germany. Perhaps to avoid serving in the military, he came to America about 1718. Having begun his teaching career in Germany, he continued his profession in a subscription elementary school. It was located among the Mennonites of the Skippack settlement north of Germantown, near Philadelphia in Pennsylvania. A subscription school was not a public school but supported by the community through tuition fees.

Teacher Dock loved his pupils and teaching, but like most Mennonites at the time he also loved farming. In 1728 he bought an additional 100 acres of farmland near Salfordville. On this farm he most likely lived for the rest of his life. He was married and had two daughters, Margaret and Catherine. His wife, whose name was probably also Margaret, died in 1761 and was buried in the Salford Mennonite Church cemetery.

Christopher Dock could not settle down to a peaceful farming life. Not long after giving up the Skippack school, he felt the "smiting hand of God" which called him back to teaching and the pupils he loved. After teaching in Germantown for four summers and after ten years of farming he resumed full-time teaching in 1738 at Skippack and Salford. He continued to teach there until his death in 1771. There is some reason to believe that Dock had left teaching for farming because he could not make ends meet with his meager teacher's salary. Even after he returned to teaching he supplemented his income by cleaning the graveyard and writing wills for people in the community.

Christopher Dock was not only one of the greatest teachers in colonial America, but also a progressive pedagogue. To know this man and teacher, one has to read his essay on pedagogy, "School Management," which he wrote in 1750. The essay reveals a gentle and loving man, an educator who devised teaching methods well ahead of his time.

Contrary to the rote learning of his day, Dock saw teaching as a divine calling, stressed individualized instruction, and emphasized character building and godliness as chief objectives. He did not coerce his pupils with physical punishment, as was the custom at the time. He sought to motivate them by treating them with respect and love and by appealing to their sense of accomplishment and human dignity.

In addition to being a successful teacher of reading, writing, and arithmetic, Dock was also an artist, illuminator, and composer of hymns. *Fraktur* writing was Dock's specialty. Fraktur was the art of illuminating beautifully penned manuscripts. These manuscripts consisted of Bible texts and mottoes penned in colored ink. Bible verses and other pious sayings thus illuminated were pinned on the walls of the schoolroom, used as copy forms for the pupils, and given as rewards to pupils for excellent work. Some of the originals of Dock's artistic work have been preserved by the Historical Society of Pennsylvania and in the Schwenckfelder Library of Pennsburg, Pennsylvania.

Dock's teaching methods had a profound influence on teachers who taught in the German schools at that time. Teachers also followed the practice of his art and used his ideas for the encouragement of pupils well into the nineteenth century. Dock's *School Management*, eventually published by Dock's pupil, Christopher Saur, Jr., found its way into many Pennsylvania-German homes.

Martin Luther said that a teacher should be able to sing well, for singing and music help to communicate knowledge and religious faith. Dock sang with his pupils and taught singing in his school. He also served as chorister in the Salford and Skippack churches. He wrote at least seven hymns himself, five of which found their way into the earliest American Mennonite hymnal, *Kleine Geistliche Harfe* (*Small Spiritual Harp*), published in 1803. It is likely, *The Mennonite Encyclopedia* suggests, that Dock's musical contribution in his area was "largely responsible for the unusual interest in singing among the Mennonite congregations of Montgomery County."

As a teacher of religion, Dock was outstanding. His Christian education was not merely tacked on to the curriculum of his school program but part of an integrated approach to education. The so-called "sacred" and "secular" aspects of education were harmoniously blended in his Christian education for life. He used religious materials such as the New Testament and hymns in his classes and began each school day with prayer and a brief worship service.

Above all, Dock lived his Christian faith, thus showing his pupils what it meant to be a Christian. Religion for Dock "was not superficial and external, but essential, and was the firm foundation for a genuinely effective program of character building. Narrow sectarianism and theological dogmatism were entirely absent; a devout and wholehearted following of Christ was his great concern" (*The Mennonite Encyclopedia*).

It is not known where Dock was buried. It was not until 1915 that a memorial stone was erected in honor of this simple yet influential teacher by the Montgomery County Historical Society in the cemetery of the Lower Skippack Mennonite Church. The inscription on this memorial stone reads, "Here Christopher Dock, who in 1750 wrote the earliest American essay on Pedagogy, taught school, and here in 1771, he died on his knees in prayer."

11

A Sunday
in Pennsylvania

*T*his story comes from Karl Goetz, a German professor. He described his visit to the conservative Mennonites in Pennsylvania shortly before World War II. (I have translated and adapted the story.)

* * *

We drove into a most beautiful county of pastures and farmland filled with orchards, clover and potato fields, and well-kept forested areas. The clean German farmyards on both sides of the road were surrounded by well-kept gardens. We hardly met an automobile. As we drove slowly, the country all around seemed to become more and more beautiful and peaceful.

The garden of Pennsylvania! I thought to myself. The little treasure chest of America—Lancaster County! The names of villages reminded me of places in Germany and the history of the people living in this county.

Arriving at the Peter Martin farm, we stepped out of the car. A vegetable garden surrounded the house, and along its fence there grew countless rosebushes. Seven generations ago the Pennsylvania Germans had brought these gardens to America. As we entered the house, I was impressed with the cleanliness and order all around. Even the broom in the hall did not stand in a corner but had its assigned place on the white-washed wall.

The man at the table was in shirt sleeves and wore a buttoned-up vest. His head and eyes radiated quiet peace and dignity. Mother Martin wore a white head covering. I felt that these simple people possessed a goodness seldom found elsewhere.

Leaving the house, we passed on the narrow country lane one horse and buggy after another, those high-wheeled wagons with black leather roofs. We drove to the church, a simple long brick building without a steeple, located on a hill among tall poplar trees. On both sides of the wide churchyard were sheds covered with sloping roofs. These sheds were used for the horses and buggies, many of which were already there when we arrived.

Inside the church it was fairly dark, for the sky this Sunday was heavily overcast. A spring storm was developing. Only slowly did my eyes become accustomed to the darkness. To the left of the room, women in bright or gray freshly pressed dresses and wearing white-laced head coverings sat on simple unpainted benches. The small girls, who sat barefooted with their mothers, looked with big eyes to where the elders sat at the table in the middle of the room.

The men sat on the right side, some in shirt sleeves. It was an unusually hot and humid day. The men's hats hung on poles fastened above the benches. The small boys sat with the men, either looking around the room or daydreaming. Some fell asleep, leaning their heads against their fathers' arms.

On the women's side there was more restlessness. From time to time a little barefooted girl would run between the rows of benches and then return to her place. Several women held their smallest children in their arms or had them sit on their laps.

I now could hear the thunder in the distance. Because of the increasing darkness, the elder at the table could hardly see the print in the book before him. He lifted the thick volume toward the sparse light which came from the small window on the side. He read slowly and with interruptions.

Then there was a sudden lightening flash, illuminating the entire room with a bright yellow light. Some children began to cry. Another man at the table rose to speak. He spoke slowly in a Pennsylvania-German dialect, a language spoken by thousands of people in the area. The language was warm in tone and similar to the language spoken in the Palatinate. Surprisingly, the language included only a few English words.

The old man's voice was full and deep. As he spoke calmly and in measured rhythm, the frightened children became quiet and content. With conviction and confidence he said, "It all comes from the Lord. He can destroy all things whenever he wishes." Then he added, "But the Lord has been most gracious to our people time and again." As if to prove him right, the darkness lifted and the old man said, "Look, he commands his sun to shine upon us again."

A mother who was cradling her child in her arms got up and walked slowly through the aisle past the table where the elders sat. The speaker smiled and nodded toward her. Mother Martin gave me a sign to follow her. We rose and followed the young mother through a side door into a room where stood a dozen or more cradles. The woman bedded her child in one of the cradles, covering it with a brightly-colored blanket. There were sleeping children in the other cradles. One baby had its thumb in its mouth.

The deep voice of the elder was heard from the meeting room. The weather had cleared. Under the tall poplars the horses were stamping with their hooves.

* * *

This idyllic portrait of a Mennonite community in Pennsylvania, written by a German "outsider" who valued the preservation of German ways in America, is no doubt one-sided and too obviously symbolic of paradise. It is important to note, however, that the community's Christian witness includes both religious faith and everyday living.

12

The Story of Christian Funk

*T*he story of Christian Funk and the Mennonites caught in the crosscurrents of the American wars of independence is a tragic one. It holds lessons from which Mennonites can learn, both positively and negatively, about what it means to be a people of peace in difficult times.

Christian Funk (1731-1811), who became the center of the first Mennonite division in America, came from well-established preacher families. Born in Franconia Township, Montgomery County in Pennsylvania, he was the son of Bishop Henry Funk.

In 1751 twenty-year-old Christian married Barbara, daughter of preacher Julius Cassel. They had nine children. About 1756 Funk was ordained by his father to the ministry; in 1769 he was confirmed as bishop. Funk became an able leader, with decided convictions and views and a potentially domineering personality.

Funk's life and ministry coincided with the revolutionary wars of independence in the American colonies. During these wars most Mennonites, consistent with their nonresistant principles, did not actively participate in the conflict. This does not mean, however, that they were politically neutral. Many sympathized with the aspirations of the colonies and hoped General Washington and his armies would win the war against Britain. Others favored the English and their king. As a result of their loyalty to the English and the royal house some of the Mennonites left America for Canada.

In addition to feelings of sympathy and loyalty for England, these Mennonite "Tories" believed strongly that rebellion against governments was always wrong. Romans 13 was their biblical guide for this. Christians were commanded to pray for governments, they believed, not rise up against them.

However, as time went on some Mennonites, including their bishops and preachers, came to believe that the colonies were not really rebels but fought for justifiable causes. When Christian Funk read the new constitution of Pennsylvania, which included freedom of conscience for minority groups like the Mennonites, he was certain that the emerging state deserved Mennonite support.

During the wars of independence Mennonites and other historic peace groups were exempt from military drills and service which were obligatory for all other citizens of Pennsylvania. The peace groups were required, however, to pay an extra sum of money, a so-called fine, for the privilege of exemption. Mennonites paid these fines with little objection, but when special war taxes were levied on all inhabitants, differences of opinion emerged among the Mennonites.

In addition to the controversial war tax of "three pounds and ten shillings," there arose this question: could Mennonites in good conscience swear a new oath of allegiance required of all Pennsylvania citizens after the 1776 Declaration of Independence? Mennonites certainly did not wish to be disloyal citizens, but they feared this new oath was not only contrary to their principle of non-swearing but would also commit them to the cause of rebellion and war.

Mennonites thus found their traditional principles assailed from many sides. They also experienced the reality of war within their previously peaceful communities. Battles took place close to their homes. The battle of Germantown, for example, was fought in the vicinity of the Mennonite meeting house, which suffered hits during the combat. The Skippack region was the location of army winter quarters. General Washington's headquarters was in the home of a Mennonite minister. And in Lancaster county horses and wagons of rich Mennonite farmers were frequently required for services during the Pennsylvania campaigns.

In 1776 an important meeting was held in Indianfield Township. Mennonites were among those present. The purpose of the meeting was to choose three men who would represent the township in a general state convention to determine whether Pennsylvania should join the other colonies in declaring independence from England.

Most of the Mennonites present stated that they were "a defenseless people and could neither institute nor destroy any government, they could not interfere in tearing themselves away from the king." Christian Funk, a strong supporter of the cause of Congress, was also present at this meeting but did not offer serious objection to the Mennonite declaration. He may have found the statement sufficiently vague to go along with.

The following year, in 1777, war taxes and the oath of allegiance became hot topics of discussion among Pennsylvania Mennonites. Christian Funk maintained that the three pounds and ten shillings tax should be paid. Other ministers, including Andrew Ziegler, a spokesman for the opposite side, believed that payment of the war tax was contrary to Mennonite nonresistance.

Christian and his brother Henry, a former Mennonite preacher in the Swamp congregation, hoped to win to their side those opposing the tax and oath of allegiance. But the other party maintained that their beliefs and convictions were based not only on their historic peace position but also the Word of God.

What follows is a summary of the meetings and exchanges that took place between Funk and the Ziegler people. The account is based largely on Funk's written and later published defense of his conduct.

Andrew Ziegler came to Christian Funk's house and informed the bishop that he, Ziegler, and another minister had recommended to the congregation that "no person should pay the tax of three pounds and ten shillings."

"I think we can pay it," Funk said.

Shortly thereafter Ziegler and Funk met again concerning the controversial issue, this time in the presence of two other ministers. Ziegler again insisted that members ought not to pay the war tax. Funk did not think Ziegler and his supporters had much influence on the congregation but it seems he was mistaken.

A few days later Andrew Ziegler came with six other ministers to Funk's house. "On seeing them approach," Funk writes, "I went towards them to salute them in peace."

Ziegler, however, stepped back and said to Funk, "I do not give you the kiss [of peace]." The other ministers followed Ziegler's example and refused Funk the customary Christian greeting.

"Are things that bad?" Funk asked. "You can still come into my house," Funk added and invited the ministers to come in.

Stepping into the house, Ziegler again asked Funk about his opinion concerning the tax.

Funk: "You already know my opinion."

Ziegler: "Do you think that paying the tax has the support of the Gospels?"

Funk: "I think so."

Ziegler: "Explain how."

Funk: "The Jews did not consider Caesar their legitimate ruler and thus thought they did not owe Caesar any tribute. When they asked Christ whether they should pay Caesar tribute, they actually tempted him in the hope that they would find a cause against him."

The bishop felt that the Gospel story was applicable to the issue at hand. He was convinced that Ziegler and his men, like the Pharisees of old, were trying to set a trap for him. Since they had refused the kiss of peace, he was certain they were his enemies.

Continuing with the Gospel story, Funk said, "Christ demanded a piece of money and asked what image and superscription it bore, to which the Jews answered 'Caesar's.' He then replied, 'Render unto Caesar that which is Caesar's and unto God that which is God's.' "

Driving his lesson home, Funk concluded, "If Christ were here, he would say, 'Give unto Congress that which belongs to Congress, and unto God what is God's.' "

Visibly agitated, Andrew Ziegler rose and exclaimed, "if I were not concerned for my life I would as soon go into the war as to pay the three pounds and ten shillings."

According to John L. Ruth in his *Maintaining the Right Fellowship*, Ziegler "seems to have meant to convey the thought that paying the war tax would be as serious a sin as breaking Christ's commandment to love one's enemy." Ruth also believes Ziegler objected to paying Congress *any* tax, not just the war tax, since Congress, according to Ziegler, was a rebellious and not legitimate government.

Ziegler and his men departed hastily, obviously angry with Bishop Funk. Funk knew that the breach between himself and the other ministers was serious. "The foundation was now laid by Ziegler and his fellow ministers," he wrote, "upon which (at a meeting held without my knowledge) they decided that I should no longer preach the gospel."

In fact, Christian Funk was excommunicated in 1778 for advocating the payment of war taxes to the revolutionary government and for refusing to oppose the swearing of allegiance to the new state. As often happens in such cases, Funk was even accused of dishonesty in business matters, thus casting grave doubts on his moral integrity.

Bishop Funk's excommunication resulted in the first schism in the American Mennonite church, with Funk establishing the congregation of the "Funk people" or "Funkites." Attempts were made, especially after the original cause of the division was no longer relevant, to bring about reconciliation and union between the two sides.

However, the attempts failed. This was largely because Christian Funk refused to admit that he had been wrong, thus effectively placing himself above the authority of the brotherhood. "I cannot give myself up," Funk said, "to the people who proclaimed me these twenty-eight years the man under the ban, and these twenty years a great thief and cheat."

In the end the ministers brought about a reconciliation. But in the five congregations in the district around Franconia, only forty-five out of one hundred sixty-three members were prepared to receive Funk back into fellowship without requiring him to recognize the authority and discipline of the church. All subsequent efforts at healing the tragic breach failed.

When Christian Funk died in 1811, his son John served as bishop of the Funkites for several decades. In 1813-14 Funk's defense of his conduct was published in both German and English under the title *A Mirror for All Mankind*. This document is the only detailed account of Funk's difficulties with the Mennonite congregations in Pennsylvania. After 1850 the Funkites ceased to exist as viable congregations. Some members transferred to the Dunkers and some to a new splinter group, the "Reformed Mennonites."

In concluding this story, John L. Ruth wrote, "This particular controversy, ironic in a group stressing 'love,' both reveals weakness and allows us to observe how a community functioned to remain faithful under threat. It failed in keeping an aggressive, independent thinker in a constructive relation to the main body . . . [and] felt constrained to deny him leadership, and then membership. His attitude was seen to be a fundamental threat to the essence of the fellowship, less, ultimately, in his political leanings than in his insistence on following his own lights whether or not the brotherhood consented. Undoubtedly he was smarter than most, if not all of his fellow members. Certainly his opponents were merciless and exaggerated in their gossipy criticism, which the church was later ready to pronounce as based on 'a fiction.' Surely resentment over his self-assertive manner became uncharitable anger."

13

The Story of a Book

On October 19, 1745, an important meeting of Mennonite ministers took place at Skippack, Pennsylvania. They had come to discuss the threatening political situation. Concerns included the war between England and France which had begun the previous year, the "rumors of war" which filled the air in the American colonies, and what all this might mean for their defenseless and peace-loving congregations.

Present at this meeting were Martin Kolb, Yellis Cassel, and Michael Ziegler of Skippack; Bishop Jacob Gottschalk of Towamencin; Dielman Kolb of Salford; and Heinrich Funk of Franconia. To meet the uncertain future, these ministers decided to write to their brothers and sisters in Amsterdam, requesting information about translating the Dutch *Martyrs Mirror* into German for use by the congregations of Pennsylvania.

Among other things they wrote, "As the flames of war appear to mount higher, no man can tell whether the cross and persecution of the defenseless Christians will not soon come, and it is therefore of importance to prepare ourselves for such circumstances with patience and resignation, and to use all available means that can encourage steadfastness and strengthen faith. Our whole community has manifested a unanimous desire for a German translation of the *Bloody Theatre of Tieleman Jansz van Braght*, especially since in this community there is a very great number of newcomers, for which we consider it to be of greatest importance that they should become acquainted with the trustworthy witnesses who have walked in the way of truth, and sacrificed their lives for it."

The writers of the letter also wished to know how much it would cost to have a thousand copies of the large book translated, printed in Holland, and shipped to the New World. They also wondered how much extra the illustrations in the *Martyrs Mirror* would cost.

The *Martyrs Mirror*, first published in 1660 in the Dutch language, was one of the most important books the Mennonites in the Netherlands had produced. The author and compiler of this stately volume of 1,290 pages was Thieleman Jansz van Braght (1625-1664), a Mennonite preacher in Dordrecht, his home town. Van Braght was a student of languages, including Latin, Greek, Hebrew, French, and German. He proved a capable defender of Mennonite principles at a time when the Mennonite faith was on the decline.

He engaged readily in debates on the streets, on ships, and wherever he had opportunity to do so. When Dutch Mennonites became more materialistic, secular, and "worldly," van Braght sided with the conservatives against the "progressive preachers." In Utrecht he even helped to depose progressive ministers, among them Willem van Maurik.

In writing and compiling the *Martyrs Mirror*, van Braght sought to inspire fellow Mennonites to renew their Christian faith and to follow their Lord more faithfully in daily living. The many stories of martyrs in the book, beginning with the early church and ending in the seventeenth century, were to remind Mennonites that they had a rich heritage of faithfulness to God and hundreds of examples of men and women ready to suffer and die for their faith. Especially the Reformation period, in which some two thousand Dutch Anabaptists were executed, edified seventeenth-century believers.

Van Braght's sources for his massive volume were the existing Dutch martyr books, particularly the *Martelaersspiegel* of 1631, stories from church history, material found in the Dordrecht and Amsterdam archives, and information obtained in Switzerland and Germany. Van Braght died in 1664, four years after publication of the *Martyrs Mirror*.

In 1685 a second edition of the *Martyrs Mirror* was published in Amsterdam, edited by an anonymous person. This edition included

104 copper engravings by Jan Luyken (1649-1712), a Mennonite artist and writer of religious and mystical poetry. Luyken's illustrations, depicting such scenes as an Anabaptist woman dying in the flames while her children watched, or Anabaptist believer Dirk Willems saving his persecutor from drowning, have inspired countless readers. Many remember the engravings long after they have forgotten the details of the stories themselves.

The Pennsylvania Mennonites had to wait two years for the Dutch answer to their letter. When the answer came it was disappointing. The Dutch suggested that a Skippack leader could translate some of the *Mirror* stories into German. Students might then copy them out in long hand for distribution to interested readers.

John L. Ruth comments in his book *Maintaining the Right Fellowship*: "The Dutch Mennonites, in an era of commercial prosperity and spiritual decline, had doubtless lost enthusiasm for their own martyr-strewn heritage, let alone the fostering of it on the strange American frontier." The American Mennonites were thus left to themselves to devise ways of translating the book for their use.

Dielman Kolb and Heinrich Funk decided to approach the Ephrata Cloister in Pennsylvania to do the *Mirror* project. Ephrata Cloister had been established by the Seventh-Day Baptists at Ephrata in Lancaster County. The group had separated from the Church of the Brethren (Dunkers) in 1735. This mystical group had organized itself into a communal life, emphasizing simplicity and a semimonastic existence. Mennonites had joined the community as well.

The community owned land. It had established an industrial center with a gristmill, sawmill, paper mill, oil mill, a tannery, and weaving and pottery factories. The residents of the cloister were teachers, musicians, artists, and makers of household articles and remedies. In 1745 the Ephrata community established one of the earliest German printing presses in America.

The Ephrata Cloister was happy to undertake the *Mirror* translation project. The terms of the agreement were generous toward the Mennonites. Peter Miller, the learned, celibate, and saintly prior of the cloister, would do the translating. Miller had come to America from Alsenborn near Kaiserslautern, Germany. He had served as a young pastor in the Reformed church at Skippack. It was rumored that Miller understood fourteen languages. Later, at the request of Congress, Miller translated the Declaration of Independence into seven European languages. Miller was well qualified to translate the *Martyrs Mirror* into German.

Just before translation was to begin, a destructive fire swept through the Ephrata Cloister on September 5, 1747. Some of the mills burned and had to be rebuilt before Miller and his assistants could begin their translation work. It took Miller three years to complete the translation. While working at his task, Miller often did not sleep more than four hours a night. During the printing process, Heinrich Funk and Dielman Kolb helped proofread and check every page for possible errors. By 1751 the huge book was published and ready for distribution.

The Ephrata edition of the *Martyrs Mirror* was an impressive book of 1,512 pages. The binding was of boards covered with leather, with corner brass mountings and two brass clasps. Some copies were issued with a copper engraved frontispiece, showing John the Baptist immersing Jesus in the Jordan River. However, since the Mennonites practiced pouring as their mode of baptism, they did not want the plate in the copies they purchased. The Dunkers, of course, liked the picture and kept it in their copies.

The book sold for 20 shillings, about $2.67 in American currency, inexpensive for such a volume. The *Martyrs Mirror* was the largest book printed in the American colonies before the Revolution in 1776.

During the revolutionary wars six American soldiers came to Ephrata with two wagons and hauled off the remaining unbound copies of *Martyrs Mirror*. The soldiers probably used some copies as wadding for their guns. The Mennonites were not amused. They believed that because of the soldiers' disrespect for the Mennonite martyrs the war would go badly for the Americans.

The Ephrata edition of the *Martyrs Mirror* proved popular, both in America and Europe. In America it went through several editions, with minor changes in 1814, 1849, 1870, 1916, and 1950. As the dates indicate, the *Mirror* was especially in demand when the world was at war and Mennonites needed to be reminded that they were a people of peace.

In Europe a reprint of the Ephrata edition appeared in 1780 in

Pirmasens, in the Palatinate, Germany. This edition was sponsored by the Amish Mennonites who lived in the vicinity of Pirmasens and preparing it for publication was the work of Elder Hans Naffziger of Essingen. This edition included the illustrations by Jan Luyken and was widely used by the Amish in the Palatinate and the Mennonites in Switzerland and Alsace-Lorraine.

An English edition of the *Martyrs Mirror*, translated from the Dutch original, appeared in 1886 in Elkhart, Indiana. Translator Joseph F. Sohm wrote in the preface to his translation, "To claim that this translation contains no errors would be simply preposterous, when all circumstances are taken into consideration; but I can truthfully say that I have conscientiously striven to furnish the reader with as correct a translation as it was in my power to give. . . . Trusting that the contemplation of the faith, the self-sacrificing zeal, and the religious fervor of these martyrs of former ages will leave its imprint for good upon the hearts of those who shall read this book, I now consign it to the hands of the printer."

Similarly J. C. Wenger, secretary of the Historical Committee of Mennonite General Conference, wrote in the publisher's preface to the fifth English edition of 1950 that "the loyalty of the Mennonite brotherhood to its historic peace principles has been tested in the first and second world wars more severely than at any time since the sixteenth century. The pressures of the contemporary culture upon the group to surrender this historic principle are strong. It is evident that vigorous efforts must be made to capture the loyalty of our youth if the Biblical doctrine of nonresistance is to be preserved."

The sentiments expressed by Sohm and Wenger have guided all the translators, editors, and sponsors of the *Martyrs Mirror* through the ages.

How reliable is the *Martyrs Mirror* as a historical record? Van Braght has been criticized by some historians on several grounds. Not only has he been charged with carelessness in his use and handling of historical material, he has also been accused of falsifying history and producing a prejudicial book. For example, the author-compiler has been criticized for including only those Anabaptist martyrs with whose theology and way of life he agreed and excluding all who did not fit what he considered "normative" Anabaptism.

Other historians, however, maintain that van Braght, while too unsuspecting and naive at times, is historically generally quite reliable. Samuel Cramer and scholars such as Ludwig Keller and W. J. Kühler considered van Braght's *Mirror* a reliable and trustworthy book.

N. van der Zijpp and Harold H. Bender wrote in the *The Mennonite Encyclopedia* concerning van Braght's alleged prejudice: "Those who criticized van Braght and accused him of omitting a large number of Anabaptists who were executed, forget that [he] only wanted to list such martyrs as gave testimony to a Biblical faith and held the strict nonresistant principles. For this reason he excluded all those Anabaptists put to death because of their religious convictions who had contacts with or were influenced by the Münsterites or other revolutionary principles."

The *Martyrs Mirror* continues to occupy a prominent place in the history and literature of Mennonites. Especially in times of prosperity and easy living, Mennonites who read the book are reminded of a past and heritage which are so easily forgotten or neglected.

14

Gold Coins
for the Journey

Christian Nafziger and his wife lived in Bavaria, Germany. The Nafzigers were hard-working farmers, but their future looked bleak and hopeless. The wars against Napoleon had devastated the countryside. The mostly Catholic neighbors were suspicious of the simple beliefs and practices of the Nafzigers and their kind—the Amish. Under these conditions Christian Nafziger found it difficult to support his family and retain hope for a better future.

The Amish followed the beliefs and practices of a young Mennonite minister in Switzerland who, toward the end of the seventeenth century, broke from the Swiss Mennonites. Jacob Amman disagreed with the rest of Mennonite elders with regard to church discipline and the frequency of celebrating the Lord's Supper. The other Mennonites were more lenient in the application of the ban and the frequency of commemorating the Lord's death. But Amman demanded that the church discipline liars and other sinners more severely, celebrate the Lord's Supper as frequently as possible, and have members show more humility in their deportment. When the differences could not be resolved, Amman and his followers founded their own group in 1694. Since then the followers of Amman have been known as Amish.

The Nafzigers wrestled for months with whether to face the risks of leaving their home and emigrating to Pennsylvania in the United

States, where some Amish from Europe had settled almost a century earlier. The prospects of an easier life were attractive, but they knew it would be difficult to leave their home, expose themselves to the dangers of travel by land and sea, and begin a difficult pioneering life in a new country.

Finally the Nafzigers decided on a kind of compromise between deciding to stay and resettling in the New World. Christian would leave his family for awhile, travel to North America, and investigate the possibilities of establishing a new home abroad. Since he had little money, Christian relied on friends and other Amish to supply him with funds for the long journey.

He traveled to Amsterdam, was helped by his friends along the way, boarded a ship bound for New Orleans, and in January of 1822 arrived in that southern United States city. But New Orleans was not his destination. It was in Pennsylvania that he hoped to find a welcome among his people and a piece of land to which he could bring his family and possibly his friends.

When Christian arrived in Pennsylvania he was well received and welcomed, but he soon knew this state would not become his new home. The price of land was so expensive that a poor peasant from Germany couldn't possibly hope to settle there. However, not all was lost. The Amish told him that there was much land in Canada, that the Canadian government was anxious to settle newcomers from Europe, and that establishing a farm there would not be as expensive as in Pennsylvania. However, Christian was also warned to be wary of unscrupulous land speculators in Canada, for some twenty years earlier land dealers had taken advantage of Mennonites there. Christian would be careful. He was eager to set out for Canada.

Supplied with money and a horse, Nafziger set out to investigate these new possibilities. In August of 1822 he arrived in the Waterloo County Mennonite settlement in what is today southern Ontario. The Mennonites, who had settled here some thirty-five years earlier, suggested that the Crown land reserved toward the west might become the site of a new settlement for the European Amish people.

So Nafziger approached Maitland, the governor of Upper Canada, who resided in York, the town which became Toronto. To Nafziger's joy, Governor Maitland agreed to sell a block of land to all the German settlers Nafziger could persuade to settle there. According to Orland Gingerich, each settler was promised fifty acres of free land provided he or she cleared a two-rod strip along the front of a two hundred-acre plot, build a cabin, and pay a small surveyor's fee. The settler, moreover, could purchase the additional one hundred fifty acres of the plot at a later date for $2.50 an acre.

Christian Nafziger was overjoyed. Both God and his fellow Mennonites had been good to him. When he began his homeward journey he was assured that his Mennonite friends in Waterloo County would do all they could to help the new Amish immigrants settle on their chosen land.

But Nafziger was a practical man and the long history of his people's dealing with government officials had taught him to be wary of promises. He thus stopped off in London to have his agreement with Governor Maitland ratified. The young Amishman even managed to see the king himself, who assured Nafziger that the governor's offer was sincere and reliable. King George IV, being of German descent, was impressed with the Bavarian. Before Nafziger left the king pressed a few gold coins into his hand, bade him goodbye, and wished him and his fellow countrymen success in the future.

The Nafziger family was unable to emigrate immediately, but the good news of Nafziger's "land find" spread rapidly throughout Bavaria, Alsace-Lorraine, and the Palatinate. The news also spread to Pennsylvania that Canada was becoming a land of promise for the Amish people. In 1824 Amish began to arrive in Canada. Eventually the Nafzigers arrived in Waterloo County as well and thus began the Amish communities in southern Ontario.

When travelers to southern Ontario see rows of horses and buggies with bearded men and women with head coverings driving to church on Sunday, they might not know Christian Nafziger opened that beautiful county for these people. To this day the people who know the Amish speak well of them and perhaps even envy their simple values and way of life.

15

Kidnapped

*T*oward the end of the eighteenth century, a God-fearing Mennonite family lived on the Pfrimmerhof in the Palatinate. They were Jost and Anna Krehbiel and their five children Jacob, Adam, Dorothea, Johannes, and Mari. With other simple and hardworking Mennonites in the area, the Krehbiels lived quiet and uneventful lives—until an unusual event disrupted their peaceful existence.

Johannes, the second-youngest of the Krehbiels, was fourteen years old when his father sent him on an errand to a village not far from home. Cheerfully Johannes started out, walking along the footpath that led through the forest. He loved strolling through the forest in summertime. He enjoyed its semidarkness and cool air; he liked to listen to the singing of birds; he loved to see rabbits, quails, and partridges crossing his path. Johannes was not afraid. He whistled a tune as he walked, and occasionally he hummed a song he had learned at home.

Since Johannes had walked to this village before, his mother did not worry about her son that day. But when evening came and Johannes was still not home, Anna became anxious. Had the boy followed a rabbit or squirrel off the path and lost his way? Could he have drowned in the pond?

She became more restless as hours passed and her son did not return. While nothing bad had ever happened to the Krehbiel children, there was talk about lawless men who terrorized farmers, stealing horses, burning down buildings, and even kidnapping children to extort money. Anna's fear for her son increased. She yearned for her husband and older two sons to come home.

When Jost Krehbiel came home from the field with his sons and a hired man, Johannes was still not home. Immediately the hired man was sent to the village to inquire whether the boy had been there. He had been there, the hired man was told, and he had started on his way back early in the afternoon. Believing something must have happened to Johannes, the men lit lanterns and set out to look for him. Anna and her daughters stayed at home, hoping and praying that no harm had come to Johannes.

After midnight the men returned without Johannes. Anna sent her daughters to bed, but she and Jost were unable to fall asleep that night. They prayed and sought comfort in reading the Bible and other devotional literature. In the end they committed their child into God's care and found peace in the hope that all would turn out for the best. Days passed without any signs of Johannes.

Several days later in the quiet and darkness of the evening, while the men were again searching for the missing boy, Anna and the girls heard someone calling outside. Anna opened the window and heard a man calling in a loud voice, "Jost! Jost!"

"What about Jost?" Anna called back.

"At the little house in the back of your yard," the voice replied, "there is a letter from your Johannes."

"But where is Johannes?" Anna asked anxiously.

"Never mind!" the male voice answered. "He is somewhere in the forest. Get the letter and do exactly as you're told!"

So Johannes was kidnapped, and the robber no doubt demanded money in exchange for the boy's life. How had this come about?

On his walk through the forest Johannes had suddenly been joined by a rather thin, pale-looking man wearing a dark-blue jacket, a light-blue vest with yellow bottoms, and a three-cornered hat. The stranger asked the unsuspecting boy questions about his father and his business and other specific details.

Johannes answered all questions, trusting the friendly man who seemed to take such interest in his family and home. Then suddenly the stranger's behavior changed. He pulled the boy by the arm deep into the forest. After leading him for awhile zigzag and in different directions, the man stopped in a thick underbrush and ordered Johannes to stand still in a certain spot.

Walking around the boy several times and mumbling hocus-pocus words, the kidnapper said with a threatening gesture, "You're standing now in a magic circle. You can't get out, and you'd better not try! If you try or make a sound, you'll die!"

Johannes was terrified. When his abductor lay down to rest, the boy sat down and sobbed quietly. Night descended, and Johannes began to see strange things and hear mysterious voices. After a while he saw lights moving in the distance. He even heard people calling his name. There it was again, much closer this time. He recognized the voices of his father and brothers.

He wanted to shout for help, but the man pulled out a knife and warned him to remain perfectly still. Then the underbrush moved, and an animal snuggled up to the boy's side. It was the Krehbiel's dog, wagging his tail at finding his young master. However, one look at the angry kidnapper caused the dog to leave and rejoin the search party. Johannes now felt completely alone and forsaken.

The next day Johannes Martin—the abductor—brought the boy some food, then meandered with him for miles through the forest. The same routine was followed for several days. One day he said to the boy, "I'll write a letter to your father, demanding money for your release. You will add a few lines, telling your father that you're dead if he doesn't pay the ransom." When the man had written the note, he forced Johannes to add his lines and sign the document. This was the letter the Krehbiels were to pick up and act on.

Eimann, a brave friend of the Krehbiels, declared his willingness to pick up the letter and act as a mediator between the family and the robber. When they opened the letter, they found a note demanding 200 pieces of gold and fifty pieces of silver in exchange for Johannes. The abductor also gave specific instructions about where and how to deposit the money. The lines and signature written by Johannes left no doubt that the boy was being held captive.

The Krehbiel family's blood froze. As much as they loved their son and were willing to pay any ransom, they did not have that much money. All they could offer the abductor was ten louis d'or (gold coins). Eimann went to the designated spot in the forest and called out to the robber, "Hey, my friend, where are you!"

"What do you want?" Martin asked under the cover of bushes.

Eimann explained the predicament in which the Krehbiels found themselves and their hope that the man would be reasonable and accept their offer. But Martin sent Eimann packing. The next day the robber called from the forest again, asking Jost to hurry or not see his son again. Eimann opened the window and told the abductor that they could offer ten gold coins, no more.

When Martin realized that he could not get more, he said, "Okay, get that money to me, and bring also bread, cheese, and a bottle of brandy. And make sure you don't poison the food!"

The kidnapper's demands were met. When Martin had the money and ascertained that the food and brandy were poison-free (he had given Johannes some of the food to eat and the brandy to drink), he let the boy go. But first he again drew a circle around him and told him not to leave for half an hour. Johannes was so afraid that he waited for a whole hour before he left the circle. Then he ran home as fast as he could. All were delighted to see Johannes unharmed and safe. His mother held her son in a long embrace and wept tears of joy. Johannes had been away for nearly two weeks.

For the Krehbiel family the ordeal had a happy ending. Not so for Johannes Martin. He was eventually apprehended and brought to justice. At his trial in Mainz, it was found that he had perpetrated the various crimes all by himself, without any accomplices. This surprised the court and the communities who had lived in fear for a long time, believing that the feared robber and arsonist was the leader of a group of bandits. Nevertheless, the court dealt severely with him, sentencing him to death by decapitation.

At the trial Johannes sat with four other boys who had been kidnapped by Martin. When Martin saw Johannes in court he said, "Well, Hannes, you're not angry with me, are you?"

Johannes replied, "No."

The Krehbiels continued to be respected members of their community. Johannes later became a merchant in Mannheim, and his brother Jacob a minister at the Weierhof Mennonite congregation. Jacob eventually emigrated to America. Krehbiel descendants lived in New York, Kansas, and California, places Mennonites moved to establish a better life for themselves and their children.

16

How to Butter Up a King

*T*here was an air of excitement among the Mennonites in the vicinity of Marienburg, Prussia. On the occasion of a royal celebration in that city, King Frederick the Great was to be present in person. During the first partitioning of Poland in 1772 the Prussian king had become their king as well. But in addition, King Frederick was known to be most tolerant in religious matters in general and well disposed toward the Mennonites in particular.

The "Ole Fritz," as the king was affectionately called by his subjects, promised to reverse the adverse treatment Mennonites had received from rulers before him. Not that King Frederick cared for the Mennonites particularly, but he knew they were obedient and hardworking people who contributed greatly to the economic well-being of the state.

How were the grateful Mennonites to receive their king during this celebration? How could they express their loyalty to him? They decided to send a delegation to Marienburg. It would represent all the Mennonites in Prussia and would present him with a gift.

Mennonite historian C. Henry Smith describes this Mennonite gesture and the gift: "The churches about Marienburg . . . presented him with an appropriate gift from the products of their farms—two well-fed oxen ready for the king's table, four hundred pounds of butter, twenty cakes of cheese, together with a large assortment of chickens and ducks."

Smith adds somewhat humorously, "This gift was evidently meant to be something more than a mere token of appreciation, however, for at the same time the king was handed a petition in which the churches asked for a confirmation of the liberties they had enjoyed under the Polish rulers, including exemption from military service."

King Frederick was pleased to receive the Mennonites and their gift. He was also happy to promise them complete religious toleration. Being an enlightened ruler and knowing what was best for his realm, he granted religious toleration to all his subjects, regardless of their religion. In fact, the king did not consider religious creeds and theological niceties that important. He believed people should be free to seek their salvation in their "own fashion." As long as his subjects were good citizens, they could believe or not believe as they pleased.

Exemption from military service was another matter. King Frederick came from a long line of soldier kings, rulers who had created Prussia by the strength of their military. Some of the previous kings had even come into conflict with the peaceful Mennonites in this regard. King Frederick must have known that one of his predecessors, the eccentric Frederick William I, had in 1723 tried to recruit some half dozen tall Mennonite fellows for his Potsdam Giants' Guard. Only when the church elders interceded on behalf of the young men and reminded the king of special privileges granted them under his predecessors did the king grudgingly release them.

King Frederick the Great was much more understanding of the Mennonites and their conscience. However, there were several things he had to take into consideration. The king knew he could not exist without an army. He needed a well-organized and loyal army for the expansion of the Prussian kingdom and in his wars against his neighbors to the south and east. Serving in the army was unpopular among his subjects. To grant military exemption to a religious minority would set a bad example and deprive his government of human resources for his wars.

How then did the king solve the problem of appeasing the Mennonites on the one hand and getting from them what he needed on the other? Smith continues the story.

"Frederick finally decided that money was as essential to a program of conquest as soldiers, and as hard to get, and the Mennonites, because of some peculiar twist in their logic . . . did not draw fine distinctions between direct and indirect service. A fairly satisfactory compromise was temporarily worked out, therefore, in the course of the negotiations during the years immediately succeeding. In 1780, the great Frederick granted the Mennonites a special charter in which they were guaranteed complete religious liberty with equal rights to carry on any kind of business, on condition, however, that they pay the annual sum of five thousand thaler for the support of the military academy at Culm."

Many Prussian Mennonites accepted this compromise and thereafter continued to support the military academy for almost a hundred years. Other Mennonites, however, remained uneasy. They began to think of emigration and a country which would respect their traditions, including nonresistance. Toward the end of the 1780s many Mennonites began their trek to southern Russia, where during the next century they established prosperous colonies.

There is another delightful story about how Mennonites expressed their appreciation to the Prussian royalty.

The year 1808 was a most difficult one for the Prussian royal house. Napoleon, the French emperor, had conquered nearly all of Europe, including West and East Prussia. According to the Treaty of Tilsit of 1807, concluded between France and Russia, Prussia not only lost many of her territories but was also reduced to half of its former population. Danzig was to be a free city, garrisoned by the French. Prussia was to be held by French forces until a heavy war indemnity was paid to France.

The Prussian royal family, residing at this time in Königsberg and Memel, evoked much sympathy from their loyal subjects. People from all walks of life sought to express their love for King Frederick William III and his queen. Among well-wishers were also the Mennonites who had lived in these territories for hundreds of years. While they were a peace-loving and nonresistant people, they supported their king and government in every way possible.

On one occasion Abraham Nickel and his wife, farmers from the Culm area, visited the royal couple and presented them with gifts, appropriate tokens of the Mennonites' sympathy. Nickel brought a sum of money and Mrs. Nickel brought a basket full of freshly-made butter. Being a simple farmer, Nickel approached the king without customary formalities, kept his hat on his head, and addressed the king with the familiar "du," not the polite form of "Sie."

"My gracious king and lord," Nickel said, "your faithful Mennonite subjects in Prussia have heard with deep sorrow about the difficulties and needs which God has sent you, your house and land. We're all most sorry about this. Therefore our congregations have decided to present you this small gift."

Handing the money to the king, Nickel continued, "I've been sent by our people, and in their name I'm asking our king and lord to accept this modest gift graciously from his true and faithful subjects." At the end of his speech Nickel added more quietly: "And we shall not cease to pray for you."

Then Mrs. Nickel, smiling, handed the queen her basket and said, "I have been told that our gracious queen likes very much good and fresh butter, and that the young princes and princesses also love fresh butter on their bread. This butter of mine is pure, good, and produced on my own farm. And since butter is not all that plentiful nowadays, I thought that you might be happy to get some. I hope that my gracious queen will not despise my small gift."

Mrs. Nickel added, "You're friendly and good, and I'm so glad to have this opportunity to meet you and speak with you face-to-face."

Such language the queen understood well. Touched and with tears in her eyes, she pressed Mrs. Nickel's hand. The queen took off her shawl and put it around the simple woman's shoulders. "As a memory to this happy occasion," the queen said to Mrs. Nickel.

The king issued a receipt for the money received. He later also returned a royal favor to the Mennonites in the form of continued privileges and greater tolerance and religious liberty.

When several years later Abraham Nickel had the misfortune of losing his house and barns through fire, the king saw to it that his farm buildings were replaced—in better condition than before! Moreover, the goodwill of the Mennonite congregations toward the Prussian rulers had left a positive mark on the king. Whenever mention was made of the Mennonites, King Frederick William III spoke well of the Abraham Nickels and their people.

17

Spies

*I*n beautiful Alsace, just south of Wissembourg, the old castle of Geisberg stood until 1940. Built by Baron von Hatzel in 1711, the castle became the home of Swiss Mennonite families as early as the first part of the eighteenth century. Among early Mennonites living at the Geisberg were persons with names such as Hirschler, Lehmann, Ehrismann, Schowalter and Böhr. Having fled persecution in Switzerland, these simple and devout people farmed the land around the Geisberg. They sought to live according to their traditional confession of faith, which included a life of nonviolence, peace, and love.

During the conflict between France and Germany in 1870-71, the Geisberg area became a war zone. The castle dwellers' peaceful life was disrupted and put to a severe test. The Böhr family (the parents, Jacob and Barbara; their two children Jean and Bärbel; and Peter, an unmarried brother to Jacob), experienced something during this war which would leave its mark for the rest of their lives. The story comes to us as told by Jacob Böhr and his daughter Bärbel (Barbara), who was about thirteen at the time.

One morning in early August of 1870, as Jacob Böhr was on his way to Wissembourg on business, the first cannon shots fired by the German artillery shattered the peace of the Geisberg. Frightened, Jacob turned and rushed home. Quickly he ordered his family to gather a few valuables and take cover in a vaulted cellar of the castle.

All might have been well had it not been for some French soldiers who also sought the safety of the same cellar. Jacob tried to explain to them that their presence might compromise the Böhrs' civilian status and neutrality. They might be hurt in the crossfire between the French and the Germans.

Jacob's fears came true. Before long German bullets passed through the small sliding window of the cellar and wounded a French soldier. Another Frenchman lifted his rifle and was about to return the fire. Recognizing the danger in which they found themselves, Jacob knocked the rifle out of the soldier's hands and persuaded the others not to shoot. Outside the shooting and explosions continued.

After a while the German army gained the upper hand and surrounded the buildings of the castle. They also came to the Böhrs' hideout and demanded that the occupants of the cellar come out and surrender. A few of the French soldiers managed to escape to the French line. Others were killed or taken prisoner by the Germans.

When the members of the Böhr family emerged from the cellar, someone in the German camp shouted, "Stop them! They are spies!" Immediately German soldiers grabbed Jacob and his brother Peter, subdued them, and tied them up.

Defending himself as well as he could, Jacob said, "We're not spies. This here is our property and home. We live here!"

But the German soldiers, not believing Jacob, beat the poor man with a rifle butt and knocked him to the ground.

When Bärbel saw what they were doing to her father, she called to her mother, "Mother, Mother, they're killing our father!"

Barbara rushed to her husband's side to help him, but a soldier hit her in the chest with his rifle and threw her back. Nothing could be done to convince the soldiers that Jacob and Peter Böhr were innocent victims. They were led away to be tried as French spies.

For the two Böhr brothers six difficult weeks now began. First they were taken to the nearby village of Altenstadt. There they were informed that they would be transported to Küstrin, east of Berlin, and tried as spies. Having left the Geisberg in a hurry and without proper clothing and food, the brothers worried about their condition. On the street of Altenstadt Jacob met an acquaintance and asked him whether he could provide him with a cap and jacket. The man went home and got the desired articles. When Jacob put on the jacket he found in a pocket a piece of bread. This bread was the brothers' only food for the next two days.

During their long train ride east Jacob and Peter were humiliated and insulted time and again by the soldiers who guarded them and by curious spectators at railway station stops.

At a stop in Landau a well-dressed gentleman walked up to the two men and shouted, "You dirty dogs! You miserable dogs! You're not worth the gunpowder, but you'll be shot anyway!" With that he took a loaf of bread and threw it against Jacob's head. Then someone threw a stone, hitting Jacob's chin.

Sometimes the brothers were ordered to get off the train and walk up and down the platform so people could see the "spies." Following similar treatment in Kassel, the prisoners were given something to eat.

"Oh God," Jacob sighed, "I would rather die of hunger than get off the train to eat." Nevertheless, Jacob and Peter had to obey orders, however humiliating the mistreatment.

Eating his soup one day, Jacob wept for the first time on this trip. It happened when a kindly looking lady approached the brothers and asked who they were and why they were so sad.

Jacob answered, "We are two brothers. They have taken us from our homes because they think we're spies. I'm doubly unhappy because I couldn't even say good-bye to my wife and my two children."

Seeking to comfort the prisoners, the woman said, "You will no doubt soon be able to return to your family." With that she turned away, weeping, and left.

Near Berlin an officer appeared and demanded that the spies get out immediately. "Follow me!" the officer barked at Jacob and Peter.

Outside the brothers again had to walk up and down the platform to be viewed by soldiers and civilian spectators. Jacob recalled the words of the psalmist: "But I am like a deaf man, I do not hear, like a dumb man who does not open his mouth." Knowing that he suffered innocently, the words from the Bible were a comfort to him. In Berlin the brothers were also displayed like museum articles, but the people there behaved more decently and showed some sympathy for the prisoners.

Arriving in Küstrin, the two men were led to an open field where an entire regiment of soldiers with mounted bayonets surrounded them. In front and behind of Jacob and Peter were placed two soldiers with loaded rifles. One shouted at them, "Just one step to the side and you're dead men!" Then a lieutenant began to hold court. The Böhr brothers tried to explain that their arrest and trial were based on a misunderstanding.

The lieutenant was not impressed but instead said bluntly, "We'll soon be through with you two. You'll be shot!"

Jacob said to the officer, "I'm not afraid. If I'm shot I'll face death bravely. But let me tell you, if there were a just court, justice would prevail, for we are innocent men."

Turning to his brother, Jacob told him to remain strong and steadfast to the end. "I think we'll have to die," he said to Peter, "but at least we'll die innocent."

After the trial the brothers were taken to the fortress and placed in separate cells. They were given little food, mostly bread and black coffee. After a while, when the guards returned their money, which had been taken away, Jacob and Peter could buy better food and improve their condition somewhat. The guards' confidence in the brothers gradually increased and things got even better. They were able to acquire better clothes and such luxuries as good coffee with milk.

But the sleeping cots were very hard, and the brothers were frequently interrogated, always separately. Each time Jacob and Peter told the truth and protested their innocence. Eventually the commandant of the fortress, half convinced his prisoners were telling the truth, wrote to the German command in France, requesting that inquiry be made into the Böhrs' case. At first the replies from France were negative and nothing could be done in favor of the prisoners.

After some time the brothers were allowed to go for walks outside, but always separately and guarded. The path they used bordered a garden belonging to a military officer. One day while Jacob walked up and down that path, he saw a woman and her servant picking pears in the garden. A girl of about seven was with the woman. Noticing the prisoner, the woman put a few pears into the

girl's apron and lifted her over the fence.

The girl ran after Jacob and called, "Spy, spy, just stop for a minute!" When Jacob turned and stopped the girl asked the guard whether she could give the man some pears.

The guard said no, but Jacob, turning to the child, said, "Yes, of course, dear child, just come here and give them to me." When the girl handed Jacob the pears he gave her a silver coin.

Overjoyed the child ran to the woman and shouted, "Grandma, look the spy gave me a silver coin!" The guard did not like what he saw and told the girl to go away.

But Jacob, knowing his rights as a prisoner, said to the guard, "Let her be, and don't rob me of the small pleasure that this innocent child is giving me!"

The guard said nothing.

The only reading material the prisoners had in their cells was a New Testament, a prayer book, and a hymnbook, sufficient no doubt for the spiritual needs of pious men like the Böhr brothers. One day when the commandant inspected the cells he suggested the prisoners might benefit from other reading, particularly from books dealing with the history of the German fatherland. Jacob replied that they did not need patriotic literature but justice.

The commandant said, "We can't do anything about that."

One evening, toward the end of their sixth week in captivity, the prisoners were preparing for the night. There was an unexpected knock at Jacob's cell door.

It was the custodian's wife. She said to Jacob, "I have good news for you. Tomorrow morning at half past four you will have to be at the railway station to travel back to the Geisberg."

In his excitement and joy Jacob cried out, "At last we're cleared and our innocence established!"

Peter was also told to be ready to leave the fortress in the morning. The two brothers were so happy they could not fall asleep that night. They got up in plenty of time, had breakfast, and at half past four boarded the train which was to take them home to their loved ones.

In the meantime, shortly before the Böhr brothers were released, the German commandant at Wissembourg notified Barbara Böhr to appear before him. He told her all he knew about her husband's situation in Küstrin. He explained that the authorities were doing everything possible to clear her husband's name of the charges against him and his brother.

When it was decided that the brothers were to be released, the Böhr family was notified that Jacob and Peter were on their way home. On September 19, 1870, the two men arrived. There was great joy, not only among the immediate members of the Böhr family, but also among their many relatives and friends at the Geisberg. However, the difficulties and anxiety which Barbara had to endure during her husband's absence took their toll on the already frail woman. Her health failed. She died in 1872, just two years after her husband's return.

In 1879 Jacob's daughter Bärbel married Heinrich Dick of the Rosenhof estate in southern Russia, thus symbolically uniting Swiss and Russian Mennonites. After his son's death Jacob also moved to Russia to be near his daughter and grandchildren. He died in Russia and was buried there. Peter Böhr later married and moved away from the Geisberg.

All that remains of the Böhr family at the Geisberg are the graves of Barbara, her son Jean, and three other children who died in infancy. The beautiful headstones overlooking the ruins of the castle and the embattled Rhine Valley were commissioned and financed by Bärbel and Heinrich Dick of Russia. Having had the joy of raising her children and seeing some of her grandchildren, Bärbel died in 1912 in Russia. This was just a few years before war, revolution, and anarchy destroyed not only the Dick's estate but also the world of the Russian Mennonites.

18

Wine-Tasting

*T*he wine produced around the village of Forst in the Palatinate is world-famous. What is not so well known, however, is that in Forst there is only one particular piece of land where this famous "Forster" grows—it is the so-called Kirchenstück or church piece.

In 1834 God granted this area a particularly good wine. People remembered that vintage for a long time and stories about this wine abounded in the Palatinate. The following account, humorous but true, deals with the '34 vintage of the Forster wine and Mennonites in the area who appreciated God's excellent gift.

About forty-five minutes from the village of Forst lies the Mennonite town of Friedelsheim. Jacob Ellenberger, a Mennonite minister, had served his Friedelsheim congregation as pastor since 1828. While everybody in Friedelsheim knew about the famous Forster wine, neither the pastor nor any of his members had ever tasted a genuine Forster wine from the Kirchenstück.

At a gathering of Pastor Ellenberger and some of his parishioners, the conversation turned to the "Forster" and its quality. Those present lamented that none of them had ever tried this wine. Surely, they reasoned, they should at least be able to taste it and determine its quality for themselves.

But how could they get a sample of this '34 vintage? The owners of the Kirchenstück were not in the habit of selling their famous wine in small quantities. And to purchase large amounts of this vintage was too expensive. They could try the wine in some hotels in Mannheim or Speyer, but they did not trust the hotels. People knew that while the label on the bottle might indicate "Forster Kirchenstück," the contents were not necessarily what the label stated.

Pastor Ellenberger and his friends devised a plan. The pastor and two of his friends, all wine experts, would pay Herr Schellhorn, part-owner of the Kirchenstück, a visit. They would tell him honestly what they had in mind, hoping he would give them a taste of the famous wine.

In the spring of 1835 when the '34 vintage was ready the three men started out for the village of Forst. At the house of Herr Schellhorn they rang the door bell. A maid appeared.

"Is Herr Schellhorn at home?" the men asked.

"Yes, he is," the maid said.

"May we speak with him?"

"Where are you from, if I may ask?"

"From nearby Friedelsheim."

"Come in. I shall tell Herr Schellhorn."

The maid went into the house; the three Mennonites waited nervously for Herr Schellhorn. The maid appeared in a few minutes and led the gentlemen into Herr Schellhorn's presence, who received them in a polite and friendly manner.

"Gentlemen," Herr Schellhorn said, "what brings you to Forst, if I may ask?"

"Please excuse our boldness, sir, but we come with a special request."

"Oh!" Herr Schellhorn said and raised his eyebrows.

"We live so close to Forst," Pastor Ellenberger said, "yet we have never had the honor to test the quality of your famous wine ourselves. As good neighbors we owe it to you and to ourselves to get to know this most noble wine grown here. We thus humbly request that you allow us to taste your '34 vintage."

"Well, well," Herr Schellhorn said, "you gentlemen wish to drink our '34 vintage!"

"It may appear thus, Herr Schellhorn," the pastor said with some embarrassment, "but I can assure you that we have not come to *drink* your wine, but merely to try it."

"I'm glad to hear that, gentlemen. Your wish shall be fulfilled," Schellhorn said and turned to the maid. "Get a light and glasses," he said. Walking toward the cellar, he said to the visitors, "Please follow me into the wine cellar."

Drawing wine and offering a glass to his guests, Schellhorn said, "I have the honor of offering you our '34 vintage."

Schellhorn left the men to themselves and walked among the wine barrels. The three friends smelled the aroma of the wine, tasted it, and rolled it around in their mouths repeatedly. They looked at each other and agreed this was not the wine they were looking for.

"Herr Schellhorn," the pastor said, "this is good wine, but we don't think it's the '34 vintage."

"Not the '34 vintage?" Schellhorn exclaimed with seeming surprise. "Perhaps I made a mistake at the barrel."

Filling another glass from a different barrel, the host said, "This time, I'm sure, there's no mistake about the wine."

Tasting the wine, the guests again came to the conclusion that it was not the famous wine. "We're most grateful to you," the pastor said to Schellhorn, "but we had expected the '34 vintage to be of greater excellence. We must have raised our expectations about your wine too high and must now correct it."

"But gentlemen," Schellhorn said, "tell me the basis of your high expectation."

"According to our taste," the pastor said, "this is a Traminer sample, a fine wine. But in the Kirchenstück, as far as we know, it is the Riesling that occupies first place."

"You're wine experts, no doubt," the host said with satisfaction. "I shall now offer you a Riesling sample."

Schellhorn left and came back with a third sample, expressing the hope that the gentlemen would find this wine to their satisfaction.

But Ellenberger again had to tell him they considered the sample to be a Rulander wine. "We may be mistaken, but as far as we know, the bouquet of the Rulander is so different from that of a Riesling that to take one for the other would happen only among persons who lack a knowledge of wines."

"Well then," Schellhorn said, "I shall bring you a fourth sample."

As soon as our sorely tried friends sipped from the fourth glass, they all knew that this was the right one. Ellenberger informed Herr Schellhorn that they considered this sample to be the '34 Riesling vintage.

"Gentlemen," Schellhorn said, "I'm glad to have met wine experts of the rarest kind. You have correctly identified the wine samples according to their kinds and qualities. Had you decided that the first sample I offered you was of the '34 vintage, I would not have offered you any other, for your judgment would have been worthless to me. I hope you'll forgive my putting you to the test.

"And now that you have passed the test so gloriously, I have the pleasure to invite you to my room where we shall drink a glass of Riesling together."

Pastor Ellenberger told this wine-tasting story often, enjoying himself as he did so and in the end praising the noble and fiery character of that wine. He also stated that there was good reason for Christ to compare himself to the vine and to use wine to symbolize his shed blood for the redemption of mankind. An excellent wine, according to Ellenberger, is so pure and noble that it can represent the new and higher life in God and the spiritual nourishment in our hearts. And since excellent wine must always remind us of the redeeming love of Christ, a person who drinks wine to excess and without giving thanks to the giver of all good things, shows little love and respect for his Savior.

19

A Volunteer to Fight Napoleon

*T*he War of Liberation had come to an end. At the Battle of Waterloo in 1815 Napoleon was at last defeated by the combined forces of the Allies. The many volunteers who had joined the armies were now returning to their loved ones. Among those coming home was a young Mennonite, David von Riesen, from Elbing-Ellerwald in West Prussia, Germany.

Von Riesen had served in the Prussian army with distinction and valor. Before he was discharged, his superiors had pinned a medal for bravery and outstanding service on his lapel. As he was approaching his hometown, he thought how proud his wife and children would be of him and of the impression he would make on his neighbors and church members.

And yet certain doubts and unease were nagging at him. Without any compulsion or pressure from anyone, he had joined the army voluntarily. At his baptism he had promised to respect and love his church and submit to all its articles of faith and life. This included the article of nonresistance and love of enemies. By joining the army he had in effect excommunicated himself from the fellowship of his congregation.

But surely the leaders would understand that times change, that their fatherland needed all the help it could get from its subjects, and that he had performed a deed of love and discharged his holy duty in a great cause. They would no doubt receive him back into the church and even honor him for what he had done.

The leaders of his church, however, thought otherwise. His med-al of bravery made no impression on them, and his argument that he had fought in a holy cause for his country did not convince them. When he told them that other Mennonite churches readmit-ted returning soldiers, they did not change their minds. When he insisted, even demanded, that they listen to him, they said some-thing about a contrite attitude, repentance, and mending his ways. Then they left.

At home things were not going well for von Riesen either. His wife and in-laws sided with the church. They advised him to submit to the leaders, acknowledge his errors, and embrace the faith of his people.

Von Riesen was not prepared to heed the counsel of his loved ones. Instead he sought to be reinstated in his congregation by way of the courts. In formal submissions to the authorities, he accused the Mennonite leadership of denying him membership in the church after serving his country faithfully and with distinction. He had to choose between two conflicting loyalties when his father-land was in great danger. And he chose what he claimed was the higher and holier duty—to serve his country. He even charged that the leaders of the church had come between him and his family, pressuring his wife to separate from him. His personal and domes-tic peace was gone, he concluded, and he faced social ostracism and economic ruin.

First the provincial, then the royal court in Berlin investigated von Riesen's charges and complaints. The German officials gathered in-formation from both sides. They even reviewed the history and tra-ditions of the Mennonites from the time of Menno Simons to the present. They investigated the life of the Mennonites in Poland and Prussia and the privileges which had been extended to them by successive kings.

When the Mennonite elders and ministers submitted their side of the case, the story began to look different. They reported that von Riesen did not really respect nor love his church; his demand to be readmitted had more to do with personal advantage than concern for spiritual matters.

Even before he joined the army, the leaders continued, von

Riesen had not led a Christian life. He had squandered his money, accumulated debts, disappeared for a while, and was later located near the Polish border. To get away from his creditors, he had volunteered to serve his country. As for meddling in von Riesen's marital affairs, von Riesen's in-laws were certainly concerned about his life, but the church had kept out of that.

By now the von Riesen affair had become an issue that concerned all the Mennonites living in West and East Prussia and in Lithuania. In their presentation of the case, the Mennonites expressed gratitude to the government for allowing them to live according to the dictates of their conscience.

They also assured the court that their nonresistance was in no way an expression of disloyalty to the state or a condemnation of those non-Mennonite citizens who believed it their sacred duty to defend their country. The principle and practice of nonresistance among Mennonites was simply an attempt to remain true to their historic understanding of the gospel. All of their members were free to join or to leave their church. And those who decided not to live by their church's practices excluded themselves from fellowship.

After all the evidence in the case was in, the royal court in Berlin ruled in favor of the Mennonite elders and ministers. Reviewing the evidence on both sides, the Prussian officials concluded that the Mennonites were honest Christians and useful citizens of Prussia who took the gospel and their religious traditions seriously. They had the right to act as they did and had in no way broken any laws of the land. Even the legal costs incurred by them during the years of this protracted case were waived. On January 24, 1818, the royal court in Berlin rejected von Riesen's suit outright.

Commenting on the von Riesen case, Russian-Mennonite historian P. M. Friesen wrote in his history, "No matter how the individual Christian may view the question of nonresistance, the steadfastness of these Mennonite preachers deserves praise from everyone." However, von Riesen's fate became the basis of a play, *Der Mennonit* (1882), in which the Mennonite convictions are misrepresented and ridiculed and the Mennonites are branded cowardly traitors.

20

For Conscience' Sake

On November 9, 1867, the North German Confederacy passed a law which annulled the Mennonite privilege of exemption from military service. This was a critical blow to the Mennonite principles and way of life, especially to the belief that as Christians they could not in good conscience serve in the army.

The German Mennonites never recovered from this blow. Just a few years later, in 1870, Mennonites volunteered to serve in the Franco-German war. In the two world wars of the twentieth century, they served in the army side by side with their German copatriots.

Anticipating the introduction of the new conscription law and hoping to sway the government in their favor, the West Prussian Mennonites sent five delegates to Berlin. The delegates, all elders, were Gerhard Penner of the Heubuden congregation, Johann Toews of the Ladekop congregation, Johann Wiebe of the Fürstenwerder congregation, Johann Penner of the Tiensdorf congregation, and Peter Bartel of the Gruppe congregation. In our story of what these men experienced in Berlin, we follow the detailed report of Elder Peter Bartel.

The five delegates traveled to the capital by train on October 23, 1867. Checking into a hotel, they made contact with several friends who had access to the authorities. These friends advised them how to proceed and whom to see. The next day, October 24, the elders appeared before the minister of war, von Roon. Elder Toews, speaking for the Mennonite delegation, asked the minister whether the new law could be reversed to accommodate the Mennonites.

The war minister said that was not in his power to grant. Instead he suggested that the Mennonites make the government an offer of some alternative service. Elder Bartel asked whether such service could be performed without carrying weapons. The minister said that side arms would have to be carried in honor of the king, although they need not be used. The delegates could not agree to that, so the war minister wanted to know more about the Mennonite principle of nonresistance. In the end he asked, "How do you feel about us who have to use weapons in war? Can we too be saved?"

"Excellency," Elder Bartel said, "with regard to serving in the army we believe as the apostle Paul instructed the Corinthians about food sacrificed to the idols. When purchasing meat on the market, the Corinthians were to take whatever was available and not ask many questions. But if they were told that the meat had been dedicated to idols, they were not to buy it, for it would be sinful to do so.

"We believe similarly with regard to waging war. We have inherited our belief in nonresistance with our mother's milk, so to speak. Our parents and spiritual leaders have taught us from the Word of God that to wage war is sinful, hence it is a matter of conscience for us. However, Your Excellency and your people have inherited from your parents the opposite. You have been taught that to wage war is necessary to defend your fatherland and is a sacred duty, hence it is not a sacrifice to the idols, as it were, nor sinful to you."

Minister von Roon was happy to hear that the Mennonites accepted him as a Christian. He told them he would do all he could to help them in their concern. He dismissed the delegates with a friendly handshake. The delegates, realizing nothing further could be achieved at the time, took the night train home.

On February 17, 1868, the five delegates received a message from Berlin, urging them to come to the capital as soon as possible. When they arrived the following day, their friends told them that the minister of war had spoken on their behalf and that now everything depended on the goodwill of the king himself, whose audience they should seek. They were further told that within the cabinet there were differences of opinion regarding the Mennonite question. The chancellor, Otto von Bismarck, vacillated in his opinion about the Mennonites' case.

In speaking with several ministers and other officials, the Mennonites got the impression that efforts were being made to minimize the effects of the new military law upon Mennonites. However, there was not much hope that they would be exempted from the law. The minister of finance even suggested that eventually the Mennonites would have to come to terms with their scruples about serving in the military.

More importantly, the delegates were told that Mennonites in Russia were divided on the question of military service and that petitions from Mennonites who wished to serve in the army had been received. Things did not bode well for the delegates. Their only hope, they thought, lay in an audience with King William I and possibly other members of the royal house.

When the delegates were at last told that the king would see them, they rushed to their hotel and dressed for the occasion. They prayed that their mission might succeed. Arriving at the royal palace, they were shown into the reception hall. Before long an adjutant opened the double doors and the king entered the hall.

Addressing the delegates, the king asked, "Children, what is your wish?"

Speaking for the group, Elder Toews said: "Your majesty, we are elders of the Mennonite congregations in the province of Prussia. We have come with regard to the new military law passed by Parliament. The law has put us into difficulties in that its application will violate our confession of faith. We and our congregations are most confident that Your Majesty will deliver us from the sad situation we are in."

The king replied, "It is certainly not my intention to burden anyone's conscience, for my fathers and I have always respected and protected your confession. However, I cannot act against the law." The king added, however, that he would find ways to bring the law into harmony with the Mennonite conscience.

Elder Toews responded that if the new law would be applied in some form to Mennonites as well, they would require some time to adjust to it and seek ways to meet the new situation. Elder Penner added that Mennonites would even be willing to pay a certain amount of money in lieu of military service, as long as their consciences were spared.

The king assured them he was not disinclined toward their concern, for they had always been faithful subjects and loyal supporters of the royal house. Elder Wiebe expressed concern that their stance not be interpreted as insubordination to the king, for he, after all, had signed the new military law.

The king said with a smile, "Each and every one has the right to petition, including yourself." After some friendly small talk about where and how the Mennonites lived, the king dismissed the delegates.

The next day, on February 26, the delegates were admitted to Crown Prince Frederick. Elder Toews spoke again for the group, requesting that the crown prince do all he could to exempt the Mennonites from the new law.

The prince replied, "But, children, that I cannot do, for even the king is subject to the law." However, he too promised to do whatever he could to lessen the effect of the law upon Mennonites.

When Elder Toews again asked for an extension of time before the new law was applied to Mennonites, the prince asked, "For what purpose?"

Elder Bartel explained, "With all due respect to Your Royal Highness, we will need some time to sell our possessions before we emigrate. We do not wish to leave with just a staff in our hand!"

Apparently taken by surprise, the prince exclaimed, "Emigrate? Where to?"

When Elder Wiebe said that they had South Russia in mind, the prince said, "Well, in that case, you might as well keep the door back to Prussia for yourself and your children open, for what is happening here now will happen next in Russia—and then you will all be sorry."

The delegates assured the prince that the Mennonites would not emigrate hastily or gladly but only as a last resort. Elder Bartel then proposed that in exchange for military service Mennonites would be prepared to do hospital duties in times of peace and war, provided this service could be performed within their communities.

"Well, I hope things will turn out well," the prince said. He added, "But whatever you do, do not emigrate!" The prince then asked them about the size of the Mennonite congregations in Prussia, how old Mennonite children had to be before they were baptized, and other matters pertaining to Mennonite faith and life. He also inquired whether there might be flooding in low-lying areas, and observed that Mennonites were similar to the Moravian Brethren, whose congregations he had visited. Before dismissing the delegates, the prince shook their hands and assured them of his and the royal house's goodwill.

After their meeting with the prince, the delegates were ordered to appear before Privy-Counselor Wagner, the deputy minister of Chancellor Bismarck. In the end they were assured that their concern would be settled to their satisfaction.

The conscription issue was settled by an order of cabinet dated March 3, 1868. The order stipulated that those Mennonites who could not in good conscience serve in the military should perform noncombatant service as medical orderlies, clerks, and transport drivers. Some Mennonites, however, could not in good conscience accept such alternative services. They decided to emigrate to Kansas and Nebraska.

In Russia, meanwhile, the political situation developed as the Prussian crown prince had predicted. A universal conscription law was passed by the government in 1870. The Mennonites there also sent delegates to the imperial capital to negotiate favorable terms for themselves. In the end the majority of Russian Mennonites accepted forestry service in return for exemption from military duties. However, a sizable minority of some 18,000 persons decided to emigrate to Canada and the United States, beginning in 1874.

21

Dispute About Wigs

*T*here have been many disputes among Mennonites. These disputes were generally more about cultural and ethical matters than about issues related to theology and doctrine. From the sixteenth century on, and well into modern times, Mennonites have argued, quarreled, and even divided into factions over dress codes, how to administer congregational discipline, and what it means to live a worldly life. To this day there are groups among Mennonites who wear distinctive clothes and keep apart from what they consider "the world" and "worldly" activity.

In the Danzig congregation in 1740 a dispute arose over whether Mennonites might wear wigs, a practice common in many European countries at that time, including among Mennonites in Holland. This dispute was not just a storm in a Mennonite teacup. It threatened to disrupt the unity and Christian love between the congregation of Danzig, the country churches in Poland-Prussia, and the Dutch congregational communities.

The issue of wearing wigs arose when a Dutch Mennonite named Cornelius de Vogel Leonards moved to West Prussia and sought to join the Danzig congregation. Like most Dutch Mennonite men, Cornelius wore a wig. The West-Prussian Mennonites, however, did not go along with this eighteenth-century fashion. They rejected the practice as blatant worldliness, vanity, and pride. The elder of the Danzig congregation, Hinrich van Duehren, simply refused to admit Cornelius to the Lord's table and thus to full membership and fellowship in the congregation.

In the following years, however, many Mennonites in Danzig began to wear wigs themselves. Understandably, many members in the congregation regarded the wearing of wigs as a worldly development which definitely had to be curbed. Other members, particularly the younger people, saw nothing wrong with wearing a wig. To them the practice was merely part of the fashion of that time.

Because of ensuing tensions and disputes over the matter, the Danzig congregation discontinued celebrating the Lord's Supper together. The country congregations and the Dutch Mennonites tried to mediate the dispute, but all efforts at settling the issue and attempts at reconciliation failed. The Danzig congregation seemed headed for serious division.

The dispute took a dangerous turn when the wig wearers appealed to the city council of Danzig. They complained about the stubbornness of their elder and asked the city leaders to intervene on their behalf. Subsequently the vice-mayor scheduled a meeting with the Mennonite leaders for August 11, 1739.

As might be expected, at this meeting Elder van Duehren appealed to the Mennonite tradition and his conscience and thus refused to yield and change his mind. Since the elder was more or less alone in his opposition to wearing wigs, the city council threatened him with imprisonment. However, the elder's congregation intervened in his behalf, asking the authorities not to proceed so harshly against van Duehren. Nevertheless, the elder was placed under house arrest; he was allowed to leave his house only when church matters made it necessary.

The city leaders further advised the ministerial council to choose a co-elder who would be prepared to administer the Lord's Supper to the wig wearers as well. The suggestion was accepted. At a meeting with a few brethren Jan Donner was chosen as co-elder. Peace now seemed assured and congregational life promised to return to normal.

But a new complication arose. Jan Donner needed to be ordained for his position as co-elder—but van Duehren refused to give his blessing, saying that "what he found difficult to do, he could not burden another to do the same." The city council took this as obstinacy on the part of the elder and consequently put him under arrest in the city hall at his own cost.

But the elders of the country churches also declined to ordain Donner for the following reasons: The Danzig congregation had not asked the country elders for advice in time, the Danzig elder had been treated badly and his congregation had forsaken him, and they had elected another elder in a disorderly fashion and with just a few members present.

In this difficult situation the Danzigers turned to the Mennonites in Holland, asking them to send an elder to ordain Donner and, if possible, to remain in Danzig to help settle the dispute. Eventually it was agreed that Adran Koenen, minister of the Hazerwoude congregation, would go to Danzig and do whatever was possible to reconcile the factions.

In the meantime Donner died suddenly, leaving the difficult task to the Dutch Koenen. Koenen managed to settle the dispute, with the result that on October 2, 1740, the entire Danzig congregation celebrated the Lord's Supper together. Elder van Duehren was set free and allowed to act as elder in cooperation with Koenen. It was further agreed that whenever van Duehren administered the Lord's Supper, the wig wearers could absent themselves. This compromise remained in effect until Koenen returned to Holland and his place was taken by another minister at the end of 1741.

What caused the characters in this tragicomedy to act the way they did? What lesson can be drawn from this episode?

The reasons for Elder van Duehren's actions were both obvious and somewhat hidden. It was obvious that in his appeal to tradition he was right. His father had served the Danzig congregation for many years, and he himself had been elder there for decades. He was thus disinclined toward innovations that would affect the customary life of his members. His two sons and several friends in the congregation supported the elder in his rigid position.

What was not so apparent was that van Duehren showed a tendency of "lording it over" other members and ministers in Danzig. At one of the brotherhood meetings he declared that he would maintain his position "even if the entire congregation were to think otherwise." He rejected the mediation attempts of his fellow ministers because this would have diminished his authority.

The position of the country churches appears in a more favorable light. They pointed out that the wearing of wigs was foreign in their country, even among the nobility. Besides, they argued, they lived in a country where they were merely tolerated by the host population. It thus behooved them to deport themselves humbly and live simply. To follow Christ and his cross was incompatible with a Christian's imitating the world. To cut hair God had given for a cover, then to wear a wig was vain, arrogant, and worldly. They rejected the view that some needed to wear wigs for health reasons. They also objected to the intervention of the city council in congregational matters.

The intervention of the vice-mayor and his drastic action against van Duehren were highly unusual, notwithstanding the fact that some members of the congregation had asked him to become involved in their affairs. Both the members who asked for the city council's assistance and the vice mayor's actions broke a long-standing Mennonite principle—that state or civic government had no business in the internal affairs of the church.

The position of the Dutch Mennonites in the dispute is interesting. In Holland the wearing of wigs was customary; the Mennonites there had decided to allow old men with thin hair or receding hair lines to wear wigs. While stressing that members live humbly and simply, they regarded the wearing of wigs as a "convenient and helpful way to protect our health." They also believed that the inner life of a Christian and freedom in Christ were more important than dress codes and outward appearance.

This explains the tone of a letter D. Eekens wrote to the Danzig congregation when he heard that Cornelius de Vogel Leonards was denied the Lord's table because he wore a wig. "Dear and beloved brethren," he wrote, "is the wearing or not wearing of a little wig all that important to you, to the extent that an otherwise worthy member is disqualified from membership and the Lord's table just because he wears a wig? Where do we find such prescriptions in the laws of Christ which ought to be our guide in all things?"

Eekens concluded his letter by stating that the Dutch Mennonites did not wish to be what they were often accused of being—"a sect of thick-headed people who slavishly adhere to the views and practices of their elders and forebears."

The subject of this story and its analysis may be considered trivial by many Mennonites today. However, the question of what it means to be separate from the world is still with Mennonites, indeed with Christians everywhere. The dress codes of the Amish and Old Order Mennonites are well-known examples of how important outward appearance has been and is among the more conservative groups. Russian Mennonites who have resettled in Germany in recent years still stress that the outward appearance of their members is a sure sign of their inner Christian life.

It may well be that these groups tend toward a legalism contrary to the freedom and love found in Christ. However, those Mennonites who have adopted the fashions of society and become part of the ways of the world may have given up not only their traditional simple life and humility. They may also have lost the freedom from worldly care and independence from the things of this world.

22

A Politician

*H*ermann von Beckerath (1801-1870) of Krefeld, Germany, is known in Mennonite history mainly for speaking against German Mennonite nonresistance during the 1848 Frankfurt Parliament. *The Mennonite Encyclopedia* refers to "von Beckerath's *strange* opposition to the proposal for exemption of conscientious objectors from military service." In light of the Mennonite position of nonviolence, it indeed appears strange that an influential member of the Mennonite church would oppose an article of faith which had characterized Mennonites for over three hundred years.

Why did von Beckerath take this position? What does his view indicate about the German Mennonite congregations in the nineteenth century? In an attempt to answer these questions we must look at von Beckerath's home and community and at the political scene in Germany at that time.

The name von Beckerath was among the most common Mennonite family names in and around Krefeld. A new pastor in Krefeld around 1900 worried about how he would be able to keep all the von Beckeraths apart. He was advised, "You'll have no difficulties with that. When you meet a young girl, just address her as 'Fräulein von Beckerath.' The worst that might happen is that she will reply, 'Oh, you're no doubt confusing me with my cousin.' " Yet with all the von Beckeraths in the area, only one is included in the *Neue*

Deutsche Biographie, a biography of prominent persons. That person is Hermann von Beckerath.

Hermann von Beckerath, born December 13, 1801, was the eldest child of a prominent family in Krefeld. His father was a cheerful and humane man; his mother was pious, tactful, and good-natured—qualities which characterized their home. The French occupation (which came in the wake of the French Revolution and Napoleon's conquests) made the family and other Mennonites all the more sympathetic toward the Prussian state and its royal house. In 1830 the family decided to give up nonresistance as an article of their faith. Like many other Mennonites at the time, the von Beckeraths thought of themselves as loyal, patriotic German citizens.

Hermann had no doubts about his Mennonite faith and role in the community. Baptized and received into the congregation in Krefeld on March 26,1820, he based his faith and life on the biblical passage his pastor had given him on that occasion—"Rejoice that your names are written in heaven" (Luke 10:20).

During his later political activities he wrote to his parents, "Believe me, dear parents . . . the fact that my name is known throughout Germany humbles me. . . . The more serious my circumstances have become, the more I discover what a rich source of strength there is in a free and open access to our heavenly Father." His "childlike feeling" as a Christian, he assured his parents, helped him in all circumstances and difficulties as a public figure.

While Hermann was not highly educated formally, he read much and was influenced by German idealism, political liberalism, and a humanism which sought to combine Christian ethics and German middle-class values. In one of his speeches in 1847, he stressed, "The Christian religion is the religion of love, justice, and noble humanity." These ideals guided von Beckerath throughout his life.

In 1815 von Beckerath entered a banking firm as an apprentice. Eventually he became a leading member of the establishment. Von Beckerath, together with other Mennonites of Krefeld, soon competed successfully with the banking establishment of Köln and placed Krefeld's banking concerns on a firm foundation. When Frederick William IV ascended the Prussian throne in 1840, the bankers and business people became leaders of the liberal movement and contributed to political awareness in the Rhine regions.

As prominent participant in the Krefeld business establishment, von Beckerath's political influence extended first to his community, then to Prussia, and eventually, in 1848, to all of Germany. He associated with politicians, had audiences with the king, and was highly respected in local and national political circles.

As an outstanding member of the unified Prussian Landtag of 1847, von Beckerath made a famous speech for the rights of religious minorities within the modern state. He pointed out with convincing eloquence that it was the state's duty to grant constitutional rights, such as the vote and eligibility for membership in Parliament, to all citizens regardless of religious creed. This right was to include the Jews as well.

"The Christian character of the state is not based on the [Christian] creed," he argued, "but upon the spirit of Christianity. And the spirit of Christianity is nothing else than the spirit of true humanity, the spirit of love, and the spirit of freedom." A true Christian state, according to von Beckerath, must manifest this spirit in all its institutions and laws and allow it to develop fully. "I cannot call a state Christian if it seeks to imprison this spirit within creedal limits."

With these ideals and views, von Beckerath in 1848 entered the German Parliament, which met in the St. Paul's Church in Frankfurt on the Main. It has become known as the Frankfurt Parliament of 1848. Serving there as minister of finance, von Beckerath made an important speech in which he objected to granting special privileges to religious groups in Germany. Specifically, von Beckerath argued that Mennonites should not be exempt from military service, a practice former Prussian kings had allowed them. This was a serious blow, particularly to the West Prussian Mennonites who still sought to adhere to their historic peace principle.

When the Frankfurt Parliament discussed and debated the content of the new constitution, a non-Mennonite delegate proposed that exemption from military service should be included in its articles, particularly for such religious groups as the Mennonites.

Von Beckerath argued against the idea. "I do not deny that the proposals issue from a well-intentioned human point of view; but, gentlemen, they are based on political concepts which no longer exist. It must be remembered that since no universal military duty existed in Prussia at the time when the Mennonites received the right to withdraw from military service and as a compensation had to accept certain restrictions on their citizenship rights, the Mennonite privilege did not constitute an infraction of the right of other citizens. But when in 1808 in Prussia every able-bodied man was obligated to military service, the Mennonite exemption constituted an abnormality, and now that a free state is to be established whose strength rests upon the equality of its citizens in rights and duties, such a special privilege becomes utterly untenable. As the previous speaker, Mr. Martens, has stated, the Mennonites in Rhenish Prussia with few exceptions render military service without question, and refusal of military service is in no sense considered as an integral part of Mennonite doctrine. It is certain that in other parts of Germany the heightened appreciation of the state will result in the performance there [by Mennonites] of this first duty of the citizen. . . . I declare that it is contrary to the welfare of the fatherland to provide for any exception in the fulfillment of citizenship duties, no matter on what ground."

The view expressed by von Beckerath was not unusual among the German Mennonites at that time. The Mennonite Isaac Brons of Emden, also a delegate at the Frankfurt Parliament, believed similarly. His views were shared by his wife, Anna Brons, the author of the first Mennonite history written in German. However, the West Prussian Mennonite congregations petitioned the Frankfurt Parliament on September 14, 1848, not to endorse von Beckerath's position.

But in the final formulation of the constitution no positive results were achieved for the concerns of the nonresistant Mennonites. In the federal law of 1867 Mennonites lost their exemption from military service, although a year later they were granted the privilege of noncombatant services such as medical work and clerical duties. Those Mennonites in West Prussia who still held on to nonresistance knew they were fighting a losing battle. As a result some decided to emigrate to America. In the war between Germany and France in 1870-71 many German Mennonites served in the army, fighting for their king and fatherland side by side with other German citizens.

Hermann von Beckerath died on May 12, 1870, in some ways a disappointed man. In 1849 the constitutional work of the Frankfurt

Parliament had come to an end, with the king refusing to accept the crown from the hands of a democratically elected group of people. While von Beckerath continued to work for German unification as much as possible, he resigned from his position in Parliament.

He lived more and more for his family and community in Krefeld, reflecting in his free time on social and political issues. In 1862 he had a noteworthy audience with King William I in which he expressed his views and concerns regarding political reforms. While the king was not convinced by von Beckerath's frank talk, he thanked von Beckerath, shook his hand, and asked him to think well of him, "especially after this conversation."

The year von Beckerath died the war began which contributed to a united Germany. This was something von Beckerath had worked for all his life.

23

Gift from a Woman's Hand

Anna Brons (1810-1902) is the author of the first Mennonite history in Germany. The book, with its long title, *Ursprung, Entwickelung und Schicksale der Tauf-gesinnten oder Mennoniten in kurzen Zügen übersichtlich dar-gestellt von Frauenhand* (Origin, Development and Fate of the Mennonites Briefly Presented by a Woman), appeared in 1884. It was dedicated to her "beloved husband, Isaac Brons, deacon in the Mennonite congregation in Emden." This gift "from a woman's hand" was a significant beginning in the writing of Anabaptist-Mennonite history.

The story of Anna Brons, of the world in which she lived, and of how she came to write her history, provides interesting and instructive insights into the faith and life of the Mennonites of North Germany in the nineteenth century. Living in Emden and being part of a community of prominent Mennonites, Anna Brons symbolized the strength and weaknesses of nineteenth-century German Mennonites.

Anna was born on November 23, 1810, in Norden, North-West Germany, to her parents the Cremer ten Doornkaats. Her father had come from Holland in 1806 and founded in Norden the famous Doornkaat distillery, whose *schnapps* is still produced and sold worldwide. Her mother died at Anna's birth, with the result that Anna spent her childhood and youth in the home of her uncle, S. D. Cremer of Norden.

Since there was no Mennonite school in this city, Mennonite children attended the local Lutheran school. Being an intellectually active and curious child, Anna learned easily. She memorized the Apostles' Creed and many biblical passages, but, as she tells us, the Lutheran ideas and view of the Christian faith were not to her liking. God the Father was portrayed as far removed and Jesus Christ was pictured as sitting on the right hand of God who would someday return to judge the living and the dead.

In such an environment Anna found it difficult to love God or Jesus. The stern images of the deity were intensified when she saw two pictures in a house she visited. The one portrayed the devil with horns, tail, and horse's hooves. The other showed Christ as a lamb holding a banner with one of his forelegs. The devil tortured the damned in hell with a fork, while the lamb listened to the hallelujahs of the redeemed in heaven. After seeing these pictures young Anna was frightened and could not fall asleep. Only after a friend sang for her Claudius' famous evening song, "The moon has risen, the golden stars shine brightly in the sky," did she find peace and fall asleep.

The God Anna came to accept and love was the one described in Psalms 139 and 145 and presented in the Mennonite congregation. This God of her forebears was immediate, comforting, and loving. "I understood and responded to this love in my heart," Anna wrote. She experienced God as close to her and prepared to keep and guide her. She now felt liberated from the fear the Apostles' Creed and other images of God had caused her.

Even though Anna grew up in a Mennonite home and attended a Mennonite congregation, she did not learn about the history of the Anabaptists there. It was through books in her uncle's library that she learned about the spiritual forebears of her people. Especially Thieleman van Braght's *Martyrs Mirror*, a collection of stories and pictures portraying the suffering and death of Anabaptist men and women, made a profound impression.

Reading the Dutch text with some difficulty, Anna was deeply moved by the faith and perseverance of the sixteenth-century Christians who would rather die than deny their Lord. This rich spiritual heritage of the Mennonites inspired Anna later to write her history. Her book was to help her people, particularly the young among them, to appreciate and be guided by their past.

The Mennonite congregations in North Germany practiced Christian piety, emphasizing a rational, common-sense view of life. To be a good Christian and a useful, law-abiding citizen were one and the same. Mennonites were also good patriots, believing that their positive contribution to their community and society was part of their Christian obligations. A subjective inwardness and separation from communal and national affairs were foreign to them.

When Anna married Isaac Brons, she took for granted that she would support her husband in his political activities locally and on the national level. In fact, for both Anna and Isaac, political involvement and activity were part of their active Christian faith.

Anna and Isaac Brons contributed passionately toward the unification of Germany and fully supported the German royal house. Isaac was a delegate to the Frankfurt Parliament of 1848 and an activist in local political affairs. The correspondence between Anna and Isaac indicates how involved and German the couple was. Their love of the fatherland included their willingness to defend their country militarily as well. Most German Mennonites, like their coreligionists in Holland, had given up their traditional principle of nonresistance, believing pacifism was not an essential aspect of faith.

The worship services in Anna's congregation were simple yet informative and heartwarming. The minister did not shout his message "over the heads of the congregation," but spoke calmly, as with friends. The devil and hell were not mentioned. Stressing the love of God and love for one another, the minister was appreciated and respected by his parishioners.

Sermons and religious meditation were supplemented by so-called secular readings. Anna read the world's classical writings, including the works of German masters. She was particularly drawn to Friedrich Schiller; the first edition of his works was in her library. She also read books dealing with theology, history, science, and psychology. Anna tells us that for her there was no strict division between the content of the Bible and literature and scholarship. "Truly, scholarship and faith complement each other," she wrote.

Anna's baptism and membership in the congregation did not mean a radical break with the way she had believed and lived before. Together with other young people, she continued to enjoy life, denying herself little. Young people did what was socially acceptable and proper. Drinking wine and smoking, for example, were not prohibited by the church. Anna tells us that her husband loved to dance. However, Isaac Brons rejected card and dice playing, not because it was wrong but because such games were a waste of time and money.

In all their freedom and love of life Anna and Isaac had a deep faith which filled their life with meaning and purpose. Christianity was for both primarily a matter of ethics. Hans Denck's motto, "To know Christ is to follow him in life," was their conviction as well. The apostle Paul's theology concerning the redeeming power of Christ's death and resurrection was foreign to them. Christ was for them the prophet and teacher of eternal truths, truths which restored and promoted human dignity, freedom, and wholesome duty toward fellow human beings.

The Brons were deeply involved in the work of their congregation and community. They served human needs in Emden and beyond wholeheartedly and sacrificially. During a difficult winter they helped the unemployed. They set up soup kitchens for the poor and donated woolens and other materials for women's and children's clothes. Anna was especially involved in women's societies and organizations for the assistance of wounded soldiers. Her help extended to friends and enemies alike.

These values and a spirit of sacrifice the Brons also instilled in their nine children. Most of the children joined the Mennonite congregation and all made the love, ethical morality, and spirit of tolerance of their parents their own. Bernhard, Anna's oldest son, assisted his mother with the history of the Mennonites she began to write in her last decades of life.

In writing the history for which she is remembered, Anna Brons was influenced by several scholars, especially Ludwig Keller who toward the end of the nineteenth century had written on Hans Denck and the Anabaptist movement in general. Reading all the available primary and secondary sources and gathering the material for her work, Anna was motivated by two things in writing her Mennonite history. First was her sense of justice which compelled her to set straight the record of the misunderstood and misrepresented Mennonites.

Second, the Anabaptist Mennonite story needed to inspire the young among the Mennonites to follow the faith and values of their spiritual forebears. Anna was convinced that if a congregational community was ignorant of its past, it could not survive and prosper. A community's heritage, according to Anna, was the foundation upon which its faith and piety rested. There was thus a pedagogical purpose to the writing of her history.

Anna Brons' history has been superseded by better, more scholarly Mennonite histories in our century. Her work, however, was one of the first serious attempts to rehabilitate the maligned and persecuted Anabaptists and to help Mennonites appreciate their tradition and values. With her history Anna Brons also made the Mennonite faith relevant in her time.

In telling the Mennonite story the author was guided by the insight that the faith and life of a people are not static but develop and change according to times and circumstances. She thus believed that the German Mennonites of her time had remained faithful to the original principles of Anabaptism, even though they had altered or given up practices they no longer deemed important or relevant. Traditional nonresistance, for example, no longer applied in a modern nation state, she held, but the principle and practice of Christian love and peace remained and applied to enemies as well.

With Julia Hildebrandt we might agree that in today's world Anna Brons' view of church and state seems overly optimistic. We recognize today that a Christian's faith is often in conflict with the nature and objectives of states and power politics. We have become more skeptical of the intentions and practices of governments and the many institutions that need to be confronted and challenged with the claims of the gospel. Even the church as an institution leaves much to be desired and is in need of renewal; Anna Brons and her community were less aware of this.

Nevertheless, Anna Brons remains a shining example of a woman, wife, mother, Mennonite, and historian. Her deepest values will never become dated and her life inspires serious reflection.

24

In the
Face of Death

When the first Prussian Menno-
nites migrated to South Russia in 1789, the question was whether
the group would establish compact villages or settle individually on
separate pieces of land. Many favored individual farmsteads, for this
was how they had lived in Prussia for many centuries.

Jacob Höppner, one of the two deputies and leaders of the
Khortitza Mennonites, built his house in the so-called cherry or-
chard near the Dnieper River, some distance from the nearest farmers. Others did the same. They soon discovered, however, that living far apart from each other was not such a good idea. The defenseless Mennonites were often molested by lawless elements
from among the native population in those early years, as the following story about Jacob Höppner will illustrate.

* * *

It was late in the evening, cloudy, and very dark when Höppner
returned home from a business trip to a nearby town. Two companions were with him. As they drove into the yard, they found it
strange that no Höppner family members were to be seen or heard.
It began to rain heavily, and a sudden flash of lightning illuminated
the darkness so they could see objects around them.

As the thunder rumbled and lightning continued, Höppner and

his companions saw two strangers standing before them. One raised a large knife and the other pointed a rifle at Höppner. As the knife came down, it hit a button on Höppner's trousers, slipped off, and tore his pants. The other bandit took aim and pulled the trigger. Höppner would have been a dead man had not the rifle powder, which had become wet in the rain, failed to explode.

As Höppner appealed to his travel companions for help, he felt a severe blow of the rifle butt on his arm. Bending forward and holding his injured arm, he was unable to defend himself against the attacks of his would-be killers. Both Höppner and one of his companions, Abraham Friesen, were overcome by their assailants and bound so they could not move. The other travel companion, Peter Hildebrandt, managed to escape and get help.

Höppner soon learned what had happened. The robbers had arrived earlier in the day, broken into the house, and bound all the occupants of Höppner's home. They had taken all the valuables and armed themselves with Höppner's rifles. Then they waited for Höppner's return to extort the money they believed he carried on his person or had hidden somewhere in or near the house. They now pressed Höppner to hand over his money, threatening to kill him if he refused to comply.

In the meantime Peter Hildebrandt ran to the nearby guardhouse where an old corporal and watchman of the duke's forest lived. He informed them of Höppner's situation, then rushed to the other settlers to get help. One Mennonite settler, Peter Unger, quick-tempered and strong, grabbed his rifle and saber and mounted a horse. With Hildebrandt he galloped toward Höppner's place.

When the wounded Höppner and Friesen realized help had arrived, they resorted to a military trick and shouted, "Our men, this way!" It now suddenly dawned on the bandits that one of Höppner's travel companions had reported the incident and returned with help. They gathered quickly the most valuable things and fled, leaving behind in the rush the fourteen rubles they had found in the house.

The bandits were later apprehended and brought to justice. They were merchants from the nearby town of Alexandrovsk who knew Höppner was a man of means. To the shame of some discontented settlers, it was they who had told the merchants in the town that

Deputy Höppner had received money from the Crown for services rendered on behalf of the Mennonite settlers in South Russia.

The Höppner incident contributed in part to the founding in 1790 of the Khortitza Island colony. It also led to the colonists' request for better protection by the government. The government assigned a group of Cossacks to this task. These Cossacks were under the command of an officer who resided in Rasumovka, a town not far from Khortitza.

The Cossacks, however, were soon more of a burden to the Mennonite settlers than a help. Jacob Höppner again had to deal with the troublesome situation as his courage was tested a second time.

The officer responsible for the Cossacks came one day with several of his men to the Island to pay Deputy Höppner a friendly visit. Höppner received his guests as well as he could, inviting them into his house and setting food before them. Then while Höppner and the officer were visiting in the living room, the Cossacks in the other rooms stole valuable articles from the rest of the house.

When Höppner was told by his family what was happening, he informed the officer what his men were doing and asked him in a friendly manner to order his men to return the stolen goods. The officer, however, just laughed and did nothing.

Quickly Höppner took hold of the officer's saber, which lay on the table, put it into the heavy wooden chest, and locked it. Turning to the officer, Höppner said that the government had appointed him to protect the settlers against thievery and harm. He would now report the officer to the authorities for failing his duty.

The furious officer called his Cossacks, who were about to leave with the stolen articles. Some had left already. Obeying their officer's order, the Cossacks appeared on horseback and threatened to hit Höppner. But Höppner's companion during the first attack, Abraham Friesen, grabbed a plank and knocked one of the Cossacks off his horse, crying, "The battle is over and we've won!"

In the meantime several neighbors arrived to see what was happening at Höppner's house. The officer now wisely realized that he had failed miserably. He promised that the stolen articles would be returned and apologized for all the inconveniences he and his men had caused. Höppner returned the saber to the officer and the horsemen rode off to Rasumovka.

25

Visits from the Tsar

*F*or the Mennonites in Russia, as for so many other Russian subjects, the tsar was God's anointed leader, even God's representative on earth. They respected and loved the tsar because the Bible commanded them to pray for kings and rulers and be obedient to governments. They also were pleased that the tsars had favored the Mennonites above many other settlers who had come to the vast regions of the Russian empire.

Empress Catherine I had extended the Charter of Privileges to the Mennonites and Tsar Paul had signed it in 1800. According to the charter, Mennonites had received land and supplies to begin their life in Russia, had the freedom to establish their own schools and teach their beloved German to their children, and never had to perform military service in the imperial army. In short, the Mennonites were given complete and unending freedom to live their faith and life according to their ancient traditions.

The tsars' goodwill toward the Mennonites was evident in their awareness of the settlers' life and activities. This interest included several imperial visits to the Mennonite colonies in the south of the empire. One such visit occurred in May 1818, when Tsar Alexander I appeared in the village of Lindenau in the Molotschna colony.

Four weeks prior to the tsar's visit, an imperial officer arrived to prepare for His Highness' appearance. The minister of this village, David Hiebert, was told that the tsar also wished to enter the

Hiebert home and have breakfast with them. The couple could hardly believe that the tsar, God's anointed, would visit in their own home!

Now preparations for the noble visitor began in earnest. Four hundred horses were requisitioned for the imperial procession on that day. The colony's administrative office in Halbstadt issued one order after another to clean up and beautify the village's houses, yards, and gardens. Even the streets were to be swept and decorated with fine sand and flowers. After the streets had been prepared for the tsar's procession, no one was allowed to ride on them.

The spring weather on that May day could not have been more beautiful. The sun shone brightly from a blue sky, the birds sang, and even the dogs seemed expectant. A large crowd gathered on both sides of the street. Young and old hoped to see the emperor from close by. According to orders, the Mennonites were stationed in a tight row on the left side of the street, and the Lutherans and other persons from the neighboring district of Prischib lined up on the other side.

At last the imperial visitor appeared at the end of the village, slowly approaching the lines of hushed and respectful villagers. The tsar's train consisted of nineteen carriages. The emperor sat in the

sixth carriage, an open coach drawn by six horses. As the procession made its way through the village, the tsar greeted the people with an uplifted hand, waving gently to the right and to the left. The crowd in turn bowed humbly in silence.

Later that eventful day, minister David Hiebert wrote in his diary,

"My wife and I stood before the door of our house to welcome our noble guest. He gave the order to stop opposite our house; stepped out and with quick steps approached our door. When he stood before us my wife said:

" 'If I have found grace in the eyes of Your Imperial Majesty, I would like to offer him a small gift.' And she handed him a beautiful bouquet of flowers on a platter.

"His Majesty willingly accepted it. When we urged him to enter the house, he said:

" 'My host and hostess must enter with me.'

"A large table, decorated with two lamps and many flowers, was spread out at the top of our large room. In the lower corner near a cupboard stood a table decked with bread, butter, onions and pork. The emperor walked up and down the room with rapid strides several times.

" 'Oh,' he said, 'there is something to eat here.'

" 'Yes,' said my wife, 'if I may serve Your Imperial Majesty with this simple fare, I invite you to eat.'

"Thereupon the emperor answered: 'Yes, dear children, I want to eat here.'

"Hurriedly we adjusted the table and placed the chairs around it. The emperor would not take the seat of honor at the head of the table, however, preferring to take an ordinary chair and seating himself on the side of the table. I requested that he seat himself on the better chair. But he answered:

" 'No, my hostess shall have the place of honor.'

"Those words perplexed us, and my wife said:

" 'I am far too humble a woman to sit next to the Lord's anointed!'

" 'No, dear child,' said the emperor, taking her by the hand and leading her to the place of honor:

" 'Just be seated next to me for we are all mere humans, created equal by God!'

"I had to be seated across the table from the emperor. . . .

"His Majesty ate with apparent good appetite, drank beer and coffee, and, while eating inquired as to our circumstances in the most affable manner: how long we had been in his empire, how we liked it and whether or not we had any complaints about anyone. To this we answered:

" 'No, but we would like to thank Your Imperial Majesty for his great mercy and gracious reception of our people. We would also like to request grace and Your Majesty's protection for the future of our people. Not only for ourselves but also for our brothers-in-the-faith in Prussia, who because of the great and difficult war [against Napoleon], have come into dire straits, so that they too might find a welcome and support in your empire.'

"The emperor turned to my wife and said: 'Yes, dear child, it shall be done.'

"Upon leaving, the emperor presented my wife with a diamond ring as a souvenir of this for us so important day."

Tsar Alexander I visited the Mennonite colonies a second time in 1825. Why this personal attention, and how did the Mennonites respond to these royal favors?

Franz Isaak, a former minister in Ohrloff, writes, "The extent to which the government was concerned to expedite and bring to fruition the Mennonite responsibility of being a model in work and conduct [for other settlers to follow] can be seen by the fact that His Majesty Tsar Alexander I visited the colonies in 1818 and in 1825 [in Steinbach], which inspired the inhabitants to go about their work with joy and courage; for they saw him face-to-face who was, in so large a measure, the promoter of their well-being. His gracious condescension to enter many of the homes and his friendly fatherly encouragement filled the community with joyous confidence, and silent prayers to God and tears of gratitude followed after the much-loved father of the country."

The majority of the Mennonites perhaps did not know at the time nor cared to know about the negative feelings many Russian peasants and serfs felt about their government due to oppression by their "little fathers," the tsars. Even after the last tsar was deposed and executed in 1917, the tsars remained for many Mennonites symbols of their prosperity, peace, and home.

26

The Ban

*I*n the eighteenth century Catherine the Great, empress of Russia, invited settlers to her vast domains. Beginning toward the end of that century and continuing well into the nineteenth, Prussian Mennonites migrated to the south-Russian steppes and established a new homeland for themselves. The Mennonites were grateful for the land they received and the freedom to live their faith according to their tradition.

The Russian government, however, did not receive the industrious Mennonites for humanitarian reasons, but because it needed settlers to populate the vast steppes in the south. Moreover, the Mennonites were to become model farmers who would be good examples for others in agriculture, education, and industry.

For this purpose the Agricultural Society was established. The society was to devise ways to improve and advance agriculture among the Mennonite colonies. It was later to contribute to the progress of education and culture. Johann Cornies, a wealthy Mennonite estate owner, was appointed chairman for life of the society.

With skill, intelligence, and great effort, Cornies did all he could to make the Mennonite colonies model communities. Sheep and cattle were imported from abroad. New stock and breeds were developed. New strains of grain were adapted to south-Russian growing conditions. Forests and orchards were planted, an undertaking which eventually made the southern Ukraine a near paradise. On his extensive experimental farm in Yushanlee, Cornies grew seed-lings and trees which Mennonite farmers had to buy and plant.

Since the Russian government had bestowed on Cornies practi-cally unlimited power in the colonies, he was able to accomplish much good with his methods. Many Mennonites, especially more progressive ones, supported his measures. But there were those, especially the more conservative people and the religious leaders, who resisted Cornies' innovations and dictatorial methods.

Those who opposed Cornies saw him more as an agent of the government than an advocate for the colonies. When some minis-ters were exiled for their opposition to the Agricultural Society and to Cornies, Cornies was seen by some as an antichrist. His educa-tional and agricultural reforms were seen as factors contributing to the secularization of Mennonite life and society.

And the religious leadership feared the loss or at least weakening of its control in religious and educational institutions. Even in pure-ly agricultural and horticultural matters, Cornies' measures were re-sented by some. Cornies' demands that his plans and methods be obeyed did not sit well with Mennonites who had a long tradition of working together in communities.

From one village came persistent reports that the trees planted according to the orders of the Agricultural Society did not grow but died. Even the village mayor, called "T" in our source, confirmed that the trees that died had been planted to the exact specifications of the society and their drying up was a mystery to him. This was no doubt most surprising since the soil was very good, the saplings were of the best quality, and Mennonite farmers were known to be successful in all they tried to do.

To investigate the matter, the society sent a delegation of several persons. When the men arrived, Mayor T led them into the garden. There they saw what they would not otherwise have believed. There stood rows of trees in well-prepared soil, their bone-dry roots in the air, their branches in the ground. It had apparently never en-tered Cornies' mind to instruct that the roots be placed in the ground and the branches in the air!

The inspectors looked in disbelief first at each other, then at May-or T and the farmers with him. Without a word and with apparent contempt, they turned and left the village in a hurry.

The consequences of this practical joke played on Cornies and his society could be predicted. Since Mayor T was responsible for all nonreligious matters in his village, including that orders of the society be carried out, he was severely punished. The church in his village, of which he was a respected member, had to discipline him for disobedience and contempt of the duly authorized society and the Russian government. Indeed, Mayor T had resisted the imperial will, the tsar himself, the highest authority under God in Russia.

Mayor T was excommunicated, banned, and shunned by his congregation. He became an outcast in the community that had elected him. According to the rules, banned persons were to be avoided by their community. No one was to have anything to do with them—eating and business dealings with them were forbidden. In addition, because of the seriousness of his "crime," Mayor T was physically beaten by members of his congregation. He was ruined.

The purpose of church discipline among Mennonites was to help sinners see their failure, repent of misconduct, and be induced to return to the bosom of the church. Repentant sinners who asked forgiveness were to be pardoned and readmitted to full fellowship.

Mayor T, however, did not repent of his joke. He had, he felt, done it with the support of his villagers. Now these same persons, all members of his congregation, had turned and under pressure from the Agricultural Society excommunicated, banned, even beaten him. This was too much. Mayor T felt like a martyr.

Friends tried to persuade Mayor T to repent and confess his fault to the congregation to be reinstated. Efforts were made to make his confession as easy as possible—all to no avail.

Mayor T lived for more than thirty years after this sad incident and remained under the ban until he died. As a shunned person he lived in his own home and village as an outsider. He never ate with his Mennonite community, nor did he attend the church services.

The source of our story does not indicate whether he ate his meals separately from his wife and family. Marital avoidance, as it was called, was usually imposed on the spouse of a banned person. But when Mayor T's wife died, he attended the funeral "as one set aside." He neither ate nor drank with the mourners and no doubt left as soon as the funeral was over.

When Mayor T himself died, he was unrepentant and still banned. Our source adds, "May God judge him graciously!" Amen!

27

Sheer Madness

*M*ennonites have had a few mad or at least half-mad leaders in their nearly five centuries. They often followed such leaders to their own ruin. Münster's mad Anabaptists in the sixteenth century are by no means the only examples. Other times and conditions gave rise to strange men and women. These odd persons in turn influenced apparently sane and rational people to believe, trust, obey, and follow wherever they led them.

One such leader was Claas Epp of Hahnsau, the first and oldest Mennonite colony in the Volga region, established by his father after 1853. Like his father, Claas was efficient, had leadership ability, and was well-to-do. Being a successful farmer, he owned four farms, one in Hahnsau and three in the village of Orlov. While at times ruthlessly severe, Claas had an attractive personality and was well-liked by his fellow colonists.

During the 1870s Mennonites in Russia experienced unsettled times. A new imperial decree stipulated that in the near future Mennonites would have to perform some state service in lieu of exemption from military service, introduce more Russian into their schools, and lose their independence in educational matters. Because of these innovations, some 18,000 Mennonites eventually left Russia for Canada and the United States. The rest of the Russian Mennonites sought to come to terms with the new conditions by doing alternative service for the government and adapting to the Russian demands and ways.

Claas Epp and his followers responded to the new conditions in another way. He did not think emigration to America or compromise at home were the solutions to the problems Mennonites faced. From studying the prophetic books of the Bible, including Daniel and Revelation, and reading apocalyptic literature from Germany, Claas came to believe that the East was to be the place of refuge for Mennonites.

Following Jung-Stilling's novel *Heimweh*, Claas began to teach that Southeast Asia, some 1,500 miles from his home on the Volga, was where God would gather his own, protect them from antichrist, and eventually rapture them to himself. Opposing his own father in matters of biblical understanding and leadership, Claas Epp went so far as to set the date of Christ's return. Christ would return, according to Epp, before 1889. Those who were to be raptured had to prepare themselves for this great event.

While Epp was discredited by many of his fellow Mennonites, he was able to unify a small group of loyal followers prepared to journey with him to the East. For this purpose he called for a communion service at Hahnsau on June 25, 1880. Thirty-five families banded together, celebrated the Lord's Supper, and established themselves as the Bride Community, a body of believers dedicated to meeting their bridegroom Christ in central Asia.

The amazing thing is that intelligent and practical people were willing to follow Epp's teaching and visions. Cornelius Wall, the very image of a prophet with his long-flowing beard; Jacob Toews, a minister of ability; Franz Bartsch, an intelligent teacher; Martin Klaassen, a historian; and ministers and teachers such as Johannes and Wilhelm Penner and Hermann Jantzen—all followed Epp.

During the summer of 1880, the year in which compulsory alternative service was to be inaugurated in Russia, Epp led a small group from the Trakt on the Volga settlement on one of the most foolish, visionary, and tragic adventures in all of Mennonite history.

This exodus of Mennonites to the wild, unknown, and barren land of Turkestan in the heart of a Moslem population was fraught with hardships and sorrow. Children died on the way and had to be buried in the desert. The travelers suffered hunger and thirst and their possessions packed in horse-drawn wagons were not safe from strange raiders along the way. Nevertheless, each day the travelers stopped for religious services and sermons by their leaders. They sang such hymns as "Our Journey Leads Through the Desert" and "There's a Land That Is Fairer Than Day."

Another group, led by Elder Peters of the Molotschnaya colony, set out for east Asia at the same time. The result of these two treks was the establishment of a Mennonite settlement at Aulie Ata in Turkestan. Here the groups divided, with most of the people remaining under the saner leadership of Elder Peters. In 1881 Claas Epp took the smaller group farther on, first to Bokhara and finally to Ak Mechet, in the Khanate of Khiva. There they settled in 1882.

The Mennonite settlers in these new regions led a precarious existence. The Turkomans and other east Asian tribes were strangers to the Mennonites. Some of the nomadic people took advantage of Mennonite nonresistance, stealing from them and at times harassing them. Mennonites had to build their houses close together to protect themselves from the raiders. The Russian authorities, being far away and with little jurisdiction in those distant parts, could not provide much protection. In addition, the dry climate and unknown conditions contributed to crop failures and poverty.

In the meantime Epp's fanaticism, dreams, and visions increased with each passing year. In 1886 Epp announced that he would soon have to leave Ak Mechet with the prophet Elijah to face antichrist in the West and to confront the great "world empires." When Epp returned after a few weeks, he told his followers that Ak Mechet was the place of refuge from antichrist and that the remaining three years before the coming of Christ were important ones for the believers. He now knew the exact date of Christ's coming—March 8, 1889.

According to Fred Richard Belk, when the great day came, "Epp explained that the Lord had decided he would be the first to be caught up and then the rest would follow. A church altar table was carried outside as a throne for Epp, and when the community assembled, Epp gave a prayer and seated himself on his throne. All day the standing assembly, dressed in white robes, waited for the Lord in an attitude of fasting and prayer. At nightfall Epp told the group that the Lord had tarried; they were to return later. Although they assembled three times that day, the resurrection day came and went in bitter disappointment."

Epp had to acknowledge the mistake he had made. But his explanation merely compounded his foolishness. He pointed out that his clock, which had indicated to him "the date by pointing with its hand to the eight and nine, had caused the mistake. Actually . . . the clock was hanging on the wall lopsided; had it been straight it would have pointed to nine and one, indicating the second coming would occur in 1891 . . . he even persuaded many that they could look forward once again to a great day two years hence."

This fiasco caused some disenchanted families to leave Ak Mechet for America. Some stopped attending Epp's worship services. When in 1891 Christ's return still did not materialize, the Mennonite population of Ak Mechet dwindled even more. Still Epp continued his madness. He proclaimed God's judgment against the Bride Community and ruled the few faithful with an iron hand. Two brethren were ordered to care for the temporal needs of the Epp family so Epp himself would not have to work. Even the patient and loyal Johannes Penner began to waver in his loyalty to Epp. The break between the two men came when Epp reached the depths of his madness.

Epp proclaimed that he was the son of Christ, the fourth person of the Trinity. All future baptisms were henceforth to be done in the name of the quadruple Godhead—Father, Sons, and Holy Ghost. According to Belk, "the meek and mild Penner exploded in a fury. He knew many in the flock were naive enough to believe Epp, and so he took the offensive against his teachings."

Toward the end of the nineteenth century most of Epp's followers had left him, but a handful remained loyal almost to the end. Finally the remnant excommunicated Epp.

He died on January 19, 1913, of stomach cancer, a disappointed and lonely seventy-five-year-old man. His beloved wife, Elisabeth, had died just five days earlier.

For C. Henry Smith there is an important moral to this strange story. "This episode, one of the strangest in Mennonite annals," he writes, "deserves this rather detailed treatment here because hereby hangs a moral of interest to Mennonites. Mennonites have been unusually susceptible to unwholesome influences of this sort. A number of times undue stress upon chiliastic and apocalyptic views on the part of fanatical leaders has led to unfortunate results."

Smith and other pragmatic Mennonites living in comfortable and materialistically-minded North America find it no doubt easy to turn the Epp tragedy into a moralism against apocalypticism. It should be remembered, however, that apocalypticism is very much embedded in the biblical literature and in Anabaptist-Mennonite thought. It is part of the "blessed hope" which helped Christian believers of all time to face and overcome adversity, persecution, and death. The intent of the Claas Epp story is not to condemn apocalypticism but only its excesses.

28

Thieves and Murderers

Beginning in 1880, Mennonites from the Volga region and some from the south-Russian colonies followed Claas Epp to Southeast Asia. Believing that in the East they could live their faith, including their nonresistant ways, more easily than in the West, they embarked on a hazardous journey in search of a new homeland.

When they arrived in the predominantly Muslim region east of the Caspian Sea, they found that the natives there, many of whom still led nomadic lives, often took advantage of the Mennonites' peaceful way. Particularly the Turkoman raiders often stole their horses, broke into their homes and took what they wanted, and sometimes in broad daylight committed crimes against the defenseless Mennonites.

The young Mennonite men asked their elders whether they could arm themselves to defend their property and lives, but the elders would not allow them to carry weapons. They could carry sticks and guard their villages, but they could not violate this most important Mennonite principle. Faithfulness to this Mennonite tradition had caused them to leave their homes on the Volga and the Dnieper in the first place.

Unchecked in their lawless acts, the Turkoman raiders at last committed a most serious crime in the village of Lausan, in the Khivan district. Fred Richard Belk (in *The Great Trek of the Russian*

Mennonites to Central Asia) tells how Heinrich Abrahms was murdered for refusing to sell his wife to these nomadic men. The story which follows is told in Belk's words with some modifications and paraphrasing.

* * *

One day some of the natives from their tent village jokingly offered to buy Heinrich Abrahms' pretty young wife, Elizabeth. The joke turned into a cruel reality. The next night a band of Turkomans crept into the Abrahms home at the far end of the village to steal Elizabeth, who was pregnant at the time. Elizabeth woke up first, after she heard some noise and saw lights in the living room. Abrahms jumped out of bed and hurried to the door to frighten the robbers away. But they shot him on the spot and repeatedly stabbed his body.

Meanwhile Elizabeth hurriedly slipped out of the bedroom window to take refuge in a neighbor's home across the street. Glancing back, she saw a man she recognized from the tent village with a light in one hand and a sword in the other. He was stealthily entering the Abrahms' bedroom. Terrified, she hurried to the neighbor, hid under a bed and whispered, "Be quiet, they are coming."

When the Mennonite men arrived at the Abrahms home, the robbers had left. Abrahms was lying in a pool of blood from twenty to thirty stab wounds and a gunshot wound in his head. Many household items were missing. The men feared that Mrs. Abrahms had been kidnapped. When they found she was safe at her neighbor's, they formed a party of all the men to track down the murderers.

As the young Mennonite men were riding around the hill near their village, they surprised the bandits in the process of dividing the Abrahms' possessions.

Though unarmed, Peter Unruh angrily called, "You thieves and murderers! What are you doing?"

In an instant about fifty men surrounded Unruh and his companions. Unruh was ordered to kneel and pray to his God, for they were going to shoot him for having called them thieves and murderers.

To this Unruh responded, "Who are you and why did you mercilessly kill that young man?"

One bandit answered, "Because he did not want to let us have what we wanted."

They raised their guns. The Mennonites begged them not to shoot Unruh. At that moment a demented young man, Johann Drake, who had lost his reason over a broken engagement and the death of his parents in Germany, stepped out of the group. Drake raised Unruh to his feet and put his arms around him.

Drake looked into Unruh's eyes and said, "Brother, I will die for you!" Then he faced the Turkomans and said boldly: "Take me in place of this man. For there is no one who will miss me or cry for me, since my parents are both dead. I am alone, and I am willing to die for this man, for he has a wife and small children."

A Turkoman spokesman replied, "This we cannot do, because not only does our religion not allow it, but it is against our conscience. Go away and let us quickly kill this man who called us thieves and murderers."

Drake did not even flinch at these words. He kept his arms tightly around Unruh.

Then the bandits consulted among themselves, lowered their guns, and said, "We grant both of you your freedom and your lives."

The Turkomans mounted their horses and rode away, to the relief of the defenseless Mennonites. None of them had ever experienced anything like this incident and would never forget it.

When the local Turkoman authorities were notified of the murder, they merely suggested that the Mennonites build their houses closer together, build walls around them, and buy guns for their protection. The Russian officials could not protect the Mennonites because their garrison was too far away. Moreover, Lausan was on Khivan soil and out of their jurisdiction.

When news of the murder reached the Russian General Grottenhelm, he suggested that the Khan of the area be notified immediately. When the Mennonites reported the incident to the Khan, he ordered an investigation of the murder and robberies. He promised the Mennonites restitution for stolen property and explained that he, a staunch Uzbek, did not like Turkomans anyway. He initiated steps to shut off the Turkoman water supply in the Lausan area to bring the culprits to their knees. With the Khan's help, in a few months several robbers were captured and sent to Khiva for trial.

29

Flight Across the River

What caused 217 Mennonites in the dead of winter in 1930 to cross the Amur River into China, leaving their homes forever and risking their lives? The story of their flight is one of desperation, daring, and courage. It is an account of a people's determination to be free and to live according to conscience.

After the Revolution of 1917, the Mennonite way of life in Russia ended. Beginning in 1923, many left the Soviet Union, emigrating to Canada and Germany. When Stalin introduced his new economic programs, whereby private farms were to be converted into state collectives, and Canada made it more difficult for immigrants to enter the country, many Mennonites faced a dismal future. In addition to the economic changes, Mennonites saw their religious, educational, and cultural institutions disappear. An alien atheistic ideology was forced on them. Unable to leave the country, they looked for ways to continue their traditional existence elsewhere within the Soviet Union.

In the Amur region, in the vicinity of Blagoveshchensk, there was still sufficient land available, and the government did not as yet enforce its collectivization policy in this distant area. Thus in 1927 and 1928 Mennonites from the Ukraine and Volga regions moved there in the hope of maintaining their traditional ways a bit longer. Villages such as Shumanovka, Kleefeld, Friedensfeld, New York, and others were established. Mennonites began to feel at home again.

But the long arm of the government soon reached the Amur region as well. In 1929 Shumanovka and other villages had to unite into state-run collective farms, something the villagers had feared for some time. From now on they had to work for the state, with the government taking most of the produce for itself and leaving little for the settlers.

Jacob Siemens, the leader of the Shumanovka collective, was an intelligent and well-liked administrator. Together with other Mennonites in the administration, he devised a plan by which the entire village might escape to China and eventually reach America. The plan, however, depended on diligence, hard work, secrecy—even deception—for its success. Failure would mean imprisonment or exile to northern Siberia, perhaps even death.

Good work on the part of the Shumanovka people and a bountiful crop in 1930 made the Soviet authorities happy. The Mennonites of this village enjoyed the authorities' trust. The Shumanovka collective became a model for other villages to follow. After the harvest was in Siemens and his group suggested to the authorities that during the slack winter months the villagers might work in the forests, some 800 kilometers away. They would thus use the winter season for the good of the state. To do that, however, they needed permission to purchase horses and sleds and make other preparations for the task. The authorities were understandably surprised at the villagers' ambition and willingness to work even harder, but in the end they granted the request.

Preparation for the mass flight included buying horses and sleds and keeping their intention secret from those who could not be trusted. (There were some villagers who would have been happy to report the would-be fugitives to the GPU, the government's dreaded secret police.) Siemens and his people also had to prepare for the villagers' reception on the other side of the river. They found a Chinese guide who called himself Alexander and apparently could be trusted.

Having crossed the river before, Alexander led two Mennonites during the night to the other side and back, acquainting them with the conditions and reception among the Chinese people. As compensation for his help, Alexander demanded that upon successful completion of the flight he receive the best horse from each family. While the price seemed high, the Mennonites agreed.

The mass flight across the river was planned for December 15. When the day arrived everything was ready. Cattle had been slaughtered for meat on the way, bread and rolls were baked and packed, and valuables were securely placed in boxes. Some even packed sewing machines, milk separators, and musical instruments. It was difficult for some villagers to separate themselves from the things they owned.

Orders were given that the villagers stay in their houses and keep quiet until the signal for leaving was given. That signal might come around nine o'clock in the evening. The supper meal that evening was no longer important. Both grown-ups and children were nervous; hearts beat faster than usual. All hoped for success, but there was a real chance the flight would be foiled. Then word came that the flight had been called off for now. What had happened?

The people from New York village, who also had planned to leave on this day, sent word to Jacob Siemens that they were not ready to depart. They requested another week's time. They still needed to sell many of their things and make other preparations. They threatened to betray the flight plan if Shumanovka went ahead this night. They even placed their spies in Shumanovka to make certain no one left without them.

What were the Shumanovka people to do? To wait another week was dangerous. On December 16 Siemens and his people decided to leave that night without the New Yorkers, come what may. Ironically, the extreme cold (-40 degrees Celsius) worked in their favor. Before midnight the spies from New York left for their warm homes, believing their Shumanovka friends could not possibly leave that night.

Shortly after midnight the word was spread through the village:—"Prepare to leave!" In all households fast and mysterious activities began. Cows and other cattle were given their freedom. The large Kroeger clocks on the walls were wound up and lamps were left lighted on the tables. Women and children were packed into sleds and covered with blankets. In a short time some sixty sleds were moving in a long line through the street, with the Chinese guide Alexander ahead of them. Some young men on horseback armed with rifles rode beside and behind the nocturnal trek.

The caravan moved slowly through snow-covered fields and past several villages toward the river, a distance of about twenty kilometers. From time to time a heavily loaded sled broke down and had to be repaired in a hurry. When the trek passed the last village, Orlovka, the Mennonites were especially fearful for their lives, for here twenty border guards with a machine gun had their headquarters. The fugitives were pleasantly surprised not to see a single guard. Had Alexander, their guide, bribed the guards? The question was never answered.

When the first sleds arrived at the river, dawn was breaking in the east. The faint outlines of the "blue mountains of China," the Lesser Khingan Range to the southwest, became visible. This mountain range had fed the Mennonites' hopes and dreams of freedom while they still lived under an oppressive regime. But now there was no time to dream. They had to get their horses and vehicles safely onto the frozen river and across it, a difficult feat. The steep river bank was three meters deep, forcing the men to hold horses and sleds with all their might so as not to damage or break them. Some sleds were destroyed and had to be abandoned.

In the end all surviving vehicles were on the ice and proceeding toward the other side. As the caravan moved as fast as possible, the men on horseback cast fearful glances backward, hoping and praying no border guards would appear and begin shooting. They knew that in the past individuals and groups of fugitives had been apprehended and killed by watchful guards. This time, miraculously, all went well. The 217 Mennonites reached the other shore safely.

In the Chinese border village of Kani-Fu the fleeing Mennonites could hardly believe their good fortune. One eyewitness wrote, "Incomprehensible that we're now standing upon free soil and no longer have to be afraid of the GPU! Or is it just a hallucination? Was all that which we experienced that night a terrible and beautiful dream? But, no, it was and is no dream, but reality. We are saved! Praise and thanks be to God! We wept tears of joy."

But the joy of these people was mixed with pain and sadness. When the Aaron Warkentins took the bundle in which their two-year-old daughter was wrapped into the warm house, they discovered to their horror that the child had suffocated. Some men had their toes frozen, and when they warmed up the pain was almost unbearable. Later in Harbin these men had to have their toes amputated. In addition, while the Mennonites were happy to be in China, they still worried about being sent back through betrayal or cooperation between the Chinese police and Soviet guards.

There were, however, immediate problems to attend to. The Chinese guide now demanded his payment—the best horse from each family. But the Mennonites needed their money—and horses were money—for their further journey to Harbin. They hoped that Alexander would understand and be satisfied with fewer horses.

After some negotiation he agreed that smaller families might unite and give him a horse together. In the end he received twenty-two good horses, still a fair price for the work he had done. Moreover, the Mennonites had to pay import duties of five rubles for each horse they kept, as well as other customs duties, to the Chinese authorities. The young men also had to hand in their rifles to the police before they were allowed to travel south.

After many delays and other difficulties, the group boarded buses and trains that took them to Harbin where American and German authorities placed them in quarters prepared for refugees like them. From Harbin the refugees eventually left for the Americas, establishing new homes and beginning new lives beyond the blue mountains of China.

30

A Love Story

Klaas Peters was the most eligible bachelor in Friedensfeld. He was a handsome young man, intelligent and physically strong, well respected by both young and old, and the only heir to his parents' prosperous farm. There were few young women in the village who would not immediately have accepted his proposal of marriage. Even his slight vanity and male chauvinism were not held against him. His belief that he was number one among the young men of Friedensfeld added a certain charm to his character. His sense of humor and ability to tell jokes made him a welcome addition to young peoples' meetings and parties. Klaas was an incessant talker whose words never failed him, which made him the center of attention and focus.

One day, as a group of young people were meeting at the house of Greta Fast, Klaas was teased about whom he might marry. Not that he was getting old, but since all the girls in the colony seemed to be after him, they wanted to know what he thought on the subject. "Surely," they said, "you must know whom you like."

Laughingly Klaas said, "That I don't know. I still haven't found out. But if you all agree," he added with a twinkle in his eye, "we might find out tonight. Then the girl herself might tell you."

Anticipating another of his practical jokes, the young people allowed Klaas to proceed with whatever he had in mind.

"Listen," he said as the young men and women gathered around

him, "I'll enter the front room, close the door, then each girl in turn may come to me. I shall ask each one whether she loves me. Whoever I kiss will then tell you that I love her. Agreed?"

Laughing, the girls agreed to play Klaas's game.

One after another the girls entered the front room and emerged quickly again. Some smiled as they came out; others tried to suppress laughter. Each girl went willingly to see Klaas—except one. Anna Dick, the last girl to enter, at first refused to go.

"Klaas certainly doesn't like me, and I'm not going to be a fool!" Anna said stubbornly.

Anna Dick was the daughter of watchman Dick who lived at the end of the village. Her mother had died a few years before. Since her father's income was not sufficient to support the family, Anna worked for other well-to-do farmers, washing and helping with chores. As children Anna and Klaas had played together, but later their different stations in society had separated them.

The young people now pushed Anna to the door. She could not spoil the game, they told her. In the end she yielded and walked into the front room.

As soon as the door was closed behind Anna the young people spoke badly about her. They called her arrogant, vain, a loner. She had no reason to be stuck-up. Her innocent face and piety could not make up for her empty dowry chest.

When Anna entered the front room Klaas did with her as he had with the girls before her. "Would you agree to become my wife if I were to ask you?" he queried.

Impatiently he waited for an answer.

"No, I would not," Anna said.

Klaas was taken aback. Then as he looked at her, he saw tears rolling down her beautiful face. Her eyes shone in a way Klaas had never seen. His surprise and momentary anger subsided. There she stood before him, tall and proud, slightly smaller than he, and a figure both noble and beautiful. Her long blond braids, her blue eyes, her simple cotton dress—all these he had never noticed.

Looking her straight in the eyes, Klaas asked: "Why don't you want me, Anna?"

"Because you don't love me!"

"And what if I do?"

"You have never even looked at me after we've grown up—and now you talk of love?"

"But it can happen, don't you think?"

"I don't think so. The daughter of a village watchman can never become the wife of Klaas Peters. You can't be serious."

"But Anna, as of now I love you. I'm asking you to be my wife."

The young people outside were becoming impatient. "Well, Klaas," one called, "you're taking a long time. Is the watchman's Anna your sweetheart? Or is she refusing to let you kiss her? Open the door or else we'll come in!"

Impatiently Klaas turned to Anna: "All the girls whom I asked today said yes. Some may have been serious—but for me it was nothing but a joke. I'm serious with you, Anna. Can you love me?"

There was a loud knocking at the door. The door flew open; the young people rushed into the room. In the commotion Anna slipped out the back door and disappeared into the night.

The young people wanted Klaas to explain the long delay and Anna's whereabouts. He told them Anna had to leave for some reason, and he had just been playing practical jokes on everyone. "Let's forget the whole thing," he said.

That night Klaas could not fall asleep. He thought of Anna Dick and her refusal. The next morning at the breakfast table he told his parents he was in love and that the girl did not want him. When the parents heard that their son loved Anna Dick, they were speechless. Why would their son choose the watchman's daughter when he could have any rich girl in the colony? Finally Klaas declared that if he couldn't marry Anna he would remain a bachelor.

For weeks and months Klaas restlessly pursued the woman he loved. He tried to see her at home, at her work, anywhere, but Anna refused to engage in a serious conversation. She believed Klaas persisted only because he found her a challenge, an object to be obtained, overcome, then discarded.

Almost a year had passed since that evening in Fast's house. Many a village girl had more than once intimated to Klaas Peters that he would be a welcome suitor. Greta Fast had even told him that since her aunt had died she had inherited her farm and was now as rich as he. There was nothing to prevent their marriage.

Klaas told her in no uncertain terms, "Even if you had inherited ten farms, I still would not marry you!"

This was too much for Greta Fast. She screamed at Klaas, "Nobody wants you anyway, not even night watchman's Anna. All of us know how many boots you have worn out running after that girl." With that she walked away, head high and defiant. There was loud laughter from those who had witnessed the scene.

Klaas grabbed his cap and rushed to Anna Dick's house. He stormed into her room.

Anna was frightened. She had never seen Klaas like this. "Klaas, what has happened? Are you not well?" she asked.

"I'm not sick, but I'm crazy! For a year I've been tied to your apron strings, am taken for a fool by you and the people, and you're cold as a fish! Now either-or! Will you become my wife or not?"

Anna told Klaas to calm down and tell her what had happened before she would answer. As Klaas told her about Greta Fast, tears rolled down Anna's cheeks. She moved closer to Klaas.

"All this because of me, dear Klaas?" she asked. She put her arms around him and kissed him.

All Klaas could say was "Anna." He held her tight.

Soon after the engagement of Anna Dick and Klaas Peters was announced in church; the wedding followed a few weeks later.

For weeks the tongues of the village beauties found no rest. "That Anna. . . ." they said and much more.

But Klaas and Anna were happily married and had children. They lived on their well-kept farm until the Revolution of 1917 destroyed all, and they, like many others, had to leave their homeland forever.

31

The First Train Ride

Uncle Hermann and Aunt Anna lived in one of the Mennonite colonies in South Russia. They had been born and raised there, had married there, and had not seen much of the world beyond their village. Portly Uncle Hermann was a courageous yet simple farmer. Smooth-shaven, at least on Sundays, he had the most innocent-looking face in the world. Generally happy, he loved to tell good yarns and hear himself talk.

Aunt Anna was the opposite of her husband, although the couple got along well. She was small and skinny, fearful, always worried about this and that. When Uncle Hermann was in his element telling stories, she would merely shake her head and say, "But, Father," implying that she half believed and half disapproved of his yarns.

Their oldest daughter was married and lived in the same village. Their second daughter, Antje, also married, lived some 120 *versts* away. Once a year the parents visited Antje and her family. The youngest daughter, Lentje, and their son Gerhard looked after their farm while they were gone.

It was autumn. The harvest was completed and the winter wheat had been seeded. One day Aunt Anna said at the dinner table, "What do you think, Father, shouldn't we soon visit Antje again?"

"Well," said Uncle Hermann, as he pushed his plate aside and wiped his mouth. "I've thought about it too. There's still some plowing to be done, but then we could, of course, travel by train for once."

"By—by train!" Aunt Anna exclaimed in surprise. There was fear in her eyes. She forgot to close her mouth.

"Yes, of course." Uncle Hermann winked. "Then we won't need the horses and Gerhard can finish the plowing while we're gone."

Gerhard supported his father, saying that way there was no rush about the plowing; besides, Antje would be so happy to see her parents again.

"But, Father," Aunt Anna protested, "we've never traveled by train."

"Exactly, Mother. It's high time that we see a train and ride in it."

"But you don't even speak Russian, Father."

"What do you mean! I know a little, and when I get stuck, you, Mother, can help out," he added, knowing full well that his wife did not know Russian either.

Aunt Anna gave in. She thought of her children and grandchildren, about what she would take along for them, and how happy they would be to see them. Uncle Hermann agreed to write Antje at once that they were coming by train and they should be met at the railway station on Friday.

During the next few days preparations were made for the trip. Aunt Anna baked zwieback and other goodies. Uncle Hermann picked the best apples and pears for his grandchildren. All their things were packed into a suitcase and large basket.

Early Friday morning two brown horses were hitched to the *Droschke* and Gerhard drove his parents to the railway station, located some distance from the village. They arrived in good time, the baggage was taken to the platform, and Uncle Hermann entered the station to purchase two tickets. The price of a ticket was 92 kopeks, which meant one ruble and 84 kopeks for two. Not too expensive, Uncle Hermann thought.

The ticket counter was still closed, but there was a long line of waiting travelers. Uncle Hermann walked resolutely to the counter to make sure he would not have to wait too long. But he was told gruffly that he would have to wait his turn. Puzzled, Uncle Hermann looked at the long line, then walked slowly to the back. He waited impatiently, hoping he would get his tickets before the train came.

A long half hour later the ticket counter was still closed. At last there was the sound of a bell, indicating that the train had left the

neighboring station. Aunt Anna, who had stayed with Gerhard and the baggage on the platform, came running in and exclaimed, "Father, the bell has already sounded. The train is on the way! Don't you have the tickets yet?"

Uncle Hermann scratched his head. He explained the situation to his wife and told her to go back to the baggage.

After ten more minutes the ticket counter opened. The official began slowly to issue tickets. But, oh, how slowly it went. Each ticket was stamped, some had to be written out, then the passengers paid their money and received change.

Suddenly there was the sound of a single bell outside. Immediately Aunt Anna appeared at the door, rushed to her husband and said, "Father, the train is coming already! I can see it in the distance!"

The next minute the train pulled in, hissing as it stopped beside the train station. Uncle Hermann was now beside himself. He pushed, gesticulated, and tried to make himself understood about missing the train on account of not having tickets. But to no avail. There were still about twenty people ahead of him. Then he remembered something. If need be one could travel without a ticket. He had heard from someone that on Russian trains one could travel as a *Sajtschik* (blind passenger) and that was even cheaper.

Five minutes later the second bell sounded. This was it! Uncle Hermann left the line and rushed to the door where he collided with Aunt Anna. "Let's go," he said to her, "or else we'll still be here by tomorrow morning!"

They soon found themselves in the compartment where other passengers were already seated. The train did not move for another five minutes, but Uncle Hermann did not dare step off for the tickets, come what may. At last the third bell sounded and the train started to move.

Before long the conductor came to check the tickets. "Ladies and gentlemen, the tickets please."

With words and signs Uncle Hermann tried to explain to the conductor what had happened and that they did not have their tickets. He even got up and tried to push the railway official into the corner and press a silver ruble into his hand. Angrily the conductor thrust the passenger's hand away and walked off cursing.

What was wrong? Uncle Hermann had always been told that Russian officials were quite receptive to such "practical" friendliness. Now this! Could it be he had hit upon an honest official for once? He sat down, pondering his strange experience.

Suddenly his face was lit up. Like a flash he thrust his hand into his pocket—and sure enough! Among the several silver rubles he found a five-kopek copper piece, which was about the size of a silver ruble. Now all was clear to him. He must have pulled out the unlucky coin and without looking offered it to the conductor. The official, however, who would have much experience in these things, had seen the copper coin and become angry.

Uncle Hermann got up and placed himself by the door where the conductor should come by soon. When he did, Uncle Hermann indicated that he was sorry about the misunderstanding. He handed the conductor the silver ruble.

The conductor accepted the coin with a smile. "But at the next station," he said, "you will still have to buy your tickets."

When Uncle Hermann came back to his seat, Aunt Anna asked what the train official had said. "I did not understand everything, but I think he said that at the next station I still will have to buy tickets," Uncle Hermann said.

Aunt Anna was panic-stricken. "But then you'll have to step off the train! And if you go I'll go with you. Don't think I'll stay here by myself with all these strange people. I might lose you." Tears rolled down her cheeks.

"Okay, okay, don't cry. Perhaps we can do without the tickets.

The conductor has his silver ruble and that might do."

When the train stopped at the next station, Uncle Hermann remained in his seat. The train soon moved again and the conductor came to check the tickets. When Uncle Hermann told him he had paid him already, the man seemed to know nothing about it. Then the conductor said that payment was for the first stretch of the journey; now another payment was required.

Hesitantly Uncle Hermann gave the conductor another silver ruble. After the third station Uncle Hermann had to hand over still another ruble. He became red with rage as he did so. Fortunately they soon arrived at their destination. Through the window they saw their children, Antje and Jacob, and their two little boys. Uncle Hermann's anger began to subside.

As soon as the train came to a halt Aunt Anna stormed out and threw herself into the arms of her daughter, weeping tears of relief and joy. Then Uncle Hermann appeared in the train door, carrying in one hand the heavy suitcase and with the other dragging the basket with apples and pears behind him. He was still red in the face, mumbling something about "thievery," and "lousy officialdom." But when he came to his children and saw his grandsons tugging at his arms and legs, he wiped the sweat from his brow and said, "Well, children, we have arrived all right."

On the way to their children's village, a distance of some three *versts,* Uncle Hermann was no longer angry. He told the story of his first train ride in such a way that even Aunt Anna joined in the general merriment and laughter. And for years to come he told the story to his friends and acquaintances, always evoking boisterous laughter among them.

Aunt Anna, however, had had enough of this first train ride with Uncle Hermann. It was also their last. She would later often say, "No, no, children, the train is not for us. It is much nicer and more comfortable to travel the way we have always traveled—in a beautiful covered wagon."

32

The Canary

A young Mennonite man, single and not experienced in the ways of the world, had formerly lived in a quiet village where life was simple and earthly pleasures few. His occupation had taken him to a Russian city where he had served as a medical orderly during the war. Peter was happy-go-lucky, seeking to enjoy any forms of life that did not conflict too much with his pious upbringing. A young Russian woman caught his attention in the city. Peter fell madly in love with her and experienced the joys and sorrows that often come with love affairs.

The young woman Peter fell in love with and hoped to marry some day was Vera. She owned a canary called Trill on whom she showered all her love, to Peter's great dismay. Peter thought that if Vera paid him just ten percent of the attention she gave Trill, he would be happy. He soon discovered that the way to Vera's heart led through Trill's cage.

Trill was in some ways a peculiar bird. He would sit quietly in the corner of his cage, clean himself with his beak, ruffle his feathers, and turn his eyes mysteriously. After this prelude he would sing with a voice and joy that reminded one of springtime, happiness in faraway places, and sunshine and love. Listening to the bird's singing made one happy to be alive and grateful to God for endowing his creatures with such art and skill.

One day some mischievous boys decided to play a trick on the beautiful owner of the canary. They knocked the cage to the ground and the little door sprang open, allowing Trill to find freedom in the trees of the garden. There he perched high on a branch, a little yellow-golden spot in the evening sun's dying light. Vera was shattered by her bird's escape. Anxious to get her canary back, she ran outside, shed many tears, and from underneath the tree passionately called to Trill to come back. "Trill, my dear Trill," she pleaded, "please come to your ladylove, oh please come back to me!" But the well-meant words of the young lady meant nothing to the bird. He remained unmoved in his newfound freedom.

This seemed Peter's chance to do something significant for the woman he adored. When Vera asked him to bring back her canary, he vowed that even if the bird were to perch in the seventh heaven, he would get him back. Peter climbed the tree until, after much exertion, he was at last in reach of the bird. But as soon as he stretched out his hand, Trill flew to a tree in the neighbor's garden. Forgetting his good training, Peter cursed not only the bird but also the Canary Islands and his bad luck.

Hearing Peter's voice high up in the tree, Vera asked, "Why are you laughing up there?"

"I'm not laughing," Peter snarled. "I just wish I had climbed the neighbor's tree in the first place and waited there for the bird."

"Come down quickly," Vera urged Peter impatiently, "or else he'll fly away and we'll lose him altogether!"

"I'm coming," Peter mumbled. He clambered down, but in his haste a branch broke and Peter fell to the ground in front of Vera.

In the meantime it had grown dark. "If we don't get him soon," Peter said, "we'll never catch him. The bird is nervous and afraid. Why don't you, Miss Vera, go into the house and leave things to me. All I need is the cage and a lantern. I'll catch the canary, I promise!"

Peter took the cage and lantern and went to the neighbor's garden. He placed the cage under the tree where Trill had taken refuge and placed the lantern beside it. He opened the little door of the cage to which he attached a string, thus providing a makeshift trap. From a little distance Peter then called to the bird to come home. But Trill had no intention of obeying Peter. In fact, after a while he left the tree and disappeared several houses down the street.

Peter became desperate. What was he to do? It was not only a question of getting the canary back to please Vera; his manly pride was at stake. At that moment a thought occurred to him. *Mrs. Babiras. Yes, Mrs. Babiras is my only hope. She can help me. Mrs. Babiras. There's no other way.*

Peter returned to Vera's house, finding the young woman anxiously waiting for her precious bird. "Did you get him?" she asked as Peter entered the door. But when she saw Peter did not have the cage, she began to cry. "I'll never get my Trill back!" she wept.

Determined to carry out his deceitful plan, Peter tried to comfort Vera, lying without blushing. "Dear lady, give me an hour, and I'll have the bird back. At this moment Trill sits in front of his cage, debating whether to go home. We must give him time and not scare him. Stay here and I'll be back with the canary before long."

Vera believed Peter and wished him good luck. Picking up the cage outside, Peter ran as fast as he could through the night, stumbling repeatedly along the way. Mrs. Babiras lived about half an hour from the city. Arriving at her house, he was out of breath.

"Mrs. Babiras," he blurted as the woman opened the door, "don't be afraid. I'm not a robber nor a murderer! I have come. . . ."

"Well, what do you want, young man?" Mrs. Babiras asked. "It's ten o'clock! Quite late, don't you think?"

"Mrs. Babiras," Peter said more calmly, "I have a real problem. I need a canary! I'll give you anything you want, but, please, right now sell me one of your birds."

The woman stared at Peter and shook her head in disbelief. Finally she said, "What kind of a canary do you want? I have old or young, male or female, birds who roll their song, and many more."

"I don't care," Peter cried, "as long as it's yellow, light yellow, and has a soft and white belly. The rest doesn't matter!"

Hoping to make a good profit, Mrs. Babiras first showed Peter cages containing dozens of canaries. But they were all dark colored. Impatiently Peter asked, "Don't you have any yellow birds?"

Pointing to a small cage in the corner of the room, the woman said, "There's a beautiful yellow canary. Costs sixty rubles. Cheap. As a favor to you, I'll sell it for that."

Peter knew the price was too high, but he was delighted to see the bird. The canary resembled Trill like a twin brother. "Does he also sing?" Peter asked.

Mrs. Babiras assured Peter that the canary was the most beautiful "roller" that had ever lived. She was even prepared to write a certificate to that effect. But Peter thought it unnecessary, for he was in a hurry. He paid the price, put the bird in Trill's cage, and hurried back, proud of having accomplished the impossible.

Entering Vera's house, Peter gave the cage ceremoniously to the young woman. He announced, "Here, my dear lady, is your Trill."

If Peter thought his goddess would now shower love and gratitude on him, he was badly mistaken. Ignoring Peter, Vera took hold of the cage and exclaimed, "Oh, you got him!" She then danced with her cage like the people of Israel around the golden calf.

Peter was left standing there like a messenger who had delivered his message and now was no longer needed. He was angry and devastated. He knew the young woman would never love him. She just loved the attention he paid her and his usefulness to her, nothing else.

The next morning Peter got bad news from Vera. Trill the Second did not sing. And "the useless bird," in Vera's words, had laid a tiny egg in Trill's cage. The canary was not only not Trill, but a female bird. And female canaries, Vera said, don't sing. Vera was angry and ice cold toward Peter, despising the young man as only a beautiful, selfish, and proud person can.

Peter tried to explain and justify himself, continuing to lie through his teeth. "There must be a mistake," he told Vera. "Someone must have played a trick by placing the egg in the cage."

But Vera knew better. "You should be ashamed of yourself," she told Peter. "Your actions and lies are signs of bad breeding; you are not fit to appear in the company of ladies."

Red-faced, Peter responded angrily. The incident ended in a shouting match. Peter left quickly, never again to see the woman he had hoped to marry.

After leaving Vera's house, Peter first went to Mrs. Babiras whom he gave a piece of his mind. On the way back he thought about Trill and where he might be. He hoped the canary would survive and multiply many times. Maybe someday the new canaries would blot out Peter's bad experience by singing sweet tunes across the lands-—songs of peace, joy, and love for all.

33

Condemned to Die

*I*n the fall of 1907 F. C. Thiessen traveled to Sevastopol in the Crimea. While there he visited his friend Peter M. Friesen, the well-known Russian-Mennonite teacher, minister, and historian.

When he entered the house, Thiessen was well received by the Friesen family, but he noticed something was wrong. When he asked about P. M., he learned P. M. was home but could not be seen.

"Is he sick?" Thiessen asked.

"Yes and no. Physically he's not sick, but in his soul he is."

Thiessen was puzzled.

"You'll see for yourself," Mrs. Friesen said. "After supper we'll tell you everything." She added, "We've lived through a very difficult time."

At supper P. M. Friesen appeared. He was very pale. Normally he was exceptionally friendly, embracing his friends and happily conversing with them. But this time he hardly noticed his friend Thiessen. The meal was eaten without anyone speaking a word. Even the members of the family looked at Friesen as if he were a stranger. Friesen himself ate little, was absent-minded, and mumbled words of prayer and the name Abram Vogt. After supper Friesen retired to his room.

Olga, the Friesens' daughter, told Thiessen what had happened.

Five days earlier P. M. Friesen had received word from the local police that he should be prepared to administer holy communion to someone in prison. At about 10 o'clock that evening the police would come and take him to the prison.

Friesen was surprised and frightened. This could only mean someone was condemned to die, he thought, and the person was Mennonite. The idea that the person on death row might be a member of his people filled Friesen with dismay and fear. He discussed the matter with his wife and daughter and prayed that God would give him strength to face the situation.

Punctually at 10 o'clock there was a knock on the Friesens' door. The policeman politely apologized for the inconvenience and invited Friesen to follow him to the horse-drawn carriage. At the carriage several other police and military officers were waiting to take Friesen to the prison.

Friesen was led into a cell where several condemned men sat, each awaiting the last hour of his life. Behind a table a young man was seated, apparently writing letters. As Friesen approached the writer, he noticed that he wrote in Russian, in a beautiful hand. A large sheet of paper had been filled and another begun.

The young man looked up at Friesen and rose from his chair. Friesen looked into the man's face which was pale and drawn. The prisoner was dressed in prison clothes and his head was wrapped with a wet towel. Chains were fastened to his feet, dragging along the floor as he moved. The young man gave the impression of great gentleness and complete resignation to his fate.

Could this young man be a Mennonite? Friesen was hoping against hope that he might not be. He asked the young man first in Russian then in German and finally in Low German who he was, what he had done, and where he came from.

The prisoner said he was Abram Vogt, twenty-six years old, son of a woman who lived in one of the Mennonite villages. Together with two accomplices he had broken into a warehouse. When they were discovered by the owners, there was a shoot-out during which two men were killed and one wounded. He and his companions were apprehended by the police and sentenced to be hanged.

Vogt felt a great need to tell his story. His parents had lived at the end of the village. They were poor and did not enjoy a good reputation among the villagers. The children of the Vogts were considered badly trained and neglected by their parents. Even the children in the village did not want to have anything to do with Abram. In school he was treated as an outsider. When after seven years of schooling he tried to find a job, nobody wanted him. He left home, got into bad company, and eventually joined criminal elements in the city. Now he had come to the end of his life.

Abram Vogt told his story quietly, even gently, without the slightest nervousness or fear. He blamed no one else for his failures nor justified his actions.

Friesen was moved by the young man. At Friesen's request the officers and prison guards left the two alone, although they could see them from an adjoining room. Friesen spoke to Vogt about repentance, the grace of God, and divine forgiveness. He also quoted biblical passages and recited lines from the hymn "O sacred Head, now wounded." He then asked the young man whether he would like to partake of the Lord's Supper with him.

Vogt's eyes lighted; he said, "Yes, I would if it is possible in this place and under the circumstances." He added, "The guards have smoked up the room badly and the table here is so dirty!"

Friesen took from his bag a small white cloth, covered the table, and prepared the bread and wine. Then he spoke quietly of Christ's death for our sins. During the ceremony Vogt knelt by the table, prayed, and confessed how great a sinner he was. Friesen placed his hands on Vogt's head and asked God to bless the young man.

Vogt smiled and said, "I have wept and prayed much before you came, but I have also been happy. Now I'm very happy."

Before Friesen left he asked Vogt whether he had a wish. "Please write my mother and tell her about what has happened here," Vogt said. "I had died even before my death. I am no longer interested in the things of this world. I am as one who is rushing away!"

Abram Vogt now seemed in a hurry. His demeanor seemed to say, "At last!" Friesen felt as if the young man was urging him to leave. The men embraced and kissed, with Friesen whispering words of comfort into Vogt's ear. Vogt nodded. After one more embrace Friesen left. Shortly after midnight Vogt was executed.

It was the end of December before Friesen completed his letter to Abram Vogt's mother. Not only was he in shock because of this experience, but he also felt guilty about his and his people's failure with regard to Abram Vogt. Community, congregation, ministers, and teachers—all had failed this young man, Friesen told himself.

What Friesen perhaps did not fully realize at the time was that Abram Vogt's case symbolized the end of Mennonite isolation in imperial Russia. Around the turn of the century Mennonites were becoming part of a developing industrial society. They were thus subject to the temptations and difficulties with which such a society had to cope. The closed world of the Mennonites was ending.

Several questions arise concerning Abram Vogt's case. What exactly had Vogt done to deserve death? We know he was involved in breaking into a warehouse and a subsequent shoot-out in which persons were killed. What did the robbers intend to steal? Was the warehouse perhaps an arms depot?

If so, Vogt may have been involved with political radicals who robbed banks and sought to acquire arms with which to fight the tsarist regime. The fact that the military was involved in this case and the severity of the penalty may point in that direction. However, since we lack substantial evidence that Vogt was a revolutionary, all we can do is ask unanswerable questions.

34

The Church
Took Her Children

*T*he lot of those Mennonites of Russia who owned no land was an unhappy one. They were not respected by those who possessed land and beautiful farms, and they were discriminated against in many ways. The landless could not vote in municipal matters that affected their lives. They were treated as second-class citizens in the congregations and in civic affairs.

When the landless took their plight to the Russian government, the landowners blackmailed them before the authorities. They warned the officials that the landless were motivated by revolutionary-socialist ideas which would undermine the state's institutions and all law and order.

The Russian government, after investigating the situation of the landless, eventually ruled in favor of the poor among the Mennonites. The landless were given the right to vote, some land was assigned to them, and their human rights were protected. The Mennonite colonies themselves bought additional land and established so-called daughter colonies where the landless were settled. However, the tensions between the two classes of Mennonites remained until their Mennonite world was destroyed by the Revolution of 1917.

Cornelius and Anna Peters, a newly married couple, belonged to the landless class in late nineteenth-century South Russia. When their colony purchased a tract of land in the Yekaterinoslav area for the landless, the young couple was happy to become farmers there. They settled in Village No. 6 and began a difficult pioneering life. Their savings were quite modest. To add to their difficulties, the second year their buildings were destroyed by fire. There was no insurance on their property. Financially unable to continue farming, the Peters, together with Anna's parents, settled on a landed estate which had been rented from the nobleman Borosenko. The soil of their piece of land was very good, giving the settlers hope for the coming years. Cornelius and Anna, together with their small children, seemed to have a bright future.

Then one day tragedy struck. Cornelius became severely ill. There were no doctors nearby, and the family was too poor to secure medical help from farther away. Anna cared for her husband as well as she could. But death came to the Peters' house and took the young husband and father away. Anna was now a young widow with four small children—three daughters and a son.

After the funeral it became very quiet in the Peters' home. In their mother's presence the children were not allowed to speak of their father. It was too painful for Anna to think about the loss of her husband. She was often seen weeping, something she could not hide from her children. Her financial burdens were almost unbearable. Even if she had sold everything she owned, she still would not have been able to cover the debts on her farm. Then the Mennonite Brethren church to which she belonged decided to act on her behalf. Viewed in retrospect, one wonders whether the church acted wisely or lovingly.

At a church meeting the case of Anna Peters was discussed at some length. The congregation sought to find a way of helping the widow gain employment so she would not become a financial burden to the community. A Bible passage from 1 Timothy 5:3-16 was applied to her, supporting the view that widows need to work and keep on the straight and narrow way. In addition, Anna's children were to be taken from her and given to other families. It was thought that there would be a number of people in the community who would be willing to take in the "orphans," feed and clothe them, and train them in the right ways.

The congregation agreed to proceed according to this course of action, which would be cheaper and simpler than any other way.

Anna's son, Cornelius, wrote later in the *Mennonitische Rundschau*, "Now God had taken the widow's husband and the church her children. . . . My mother could never get over this."

For Anna a difficult life began. She sewed clothes for a living and did other jobs. Still young, she declined all offers of remarriage, remaining a widow for the rest of her life. No one in the community seemed to be concerned about the struggles and difficulties, especially the pain of a mother's heart that Anna experienced at this time. As her son Cornelius wrote: "Had God not been a father of the widows and orphans, my poor mother would not have survived."

Anna's four children also experienced the pain of separation from their mother and the feelings of loneliness that came from not having a home. Cornelius wrote that he was torn from his mother at a very tender age and thought of himself as an orphan. It slowly dawned on him that he now had no mother, no father, and no brothers and sisters.

No one seemed to care about him. He sat at the table of strangers and was merely tolerated; he was not their child. "I felt that I stood alone," he wrote. "There's no one who loves you, no one who's interested in you, and no one who will speak a friendly word to you. I felt the pain and sadness so much that I could have cried." He was pushed from one family to another, wherever there was room for the child for short periods of time.

"I no longer had a home," he recalled. "I didn't quite understand this at the time, but I had to resign myself to the situation." The same fate befell his sisters, who were slightly older than Cornelius. They too were treated as orphans and homeless children by well-meaning but insensitive people.

Eventually Cornelius and his older sister Anna were taken into the home of Cornelius Epp, a couple without children of their own. Here the two children were loved and cared for. For the first time since he had been taken from his mother, Cornelius slept in a bed. Until then he had slept in barns. The Epps were good to the two Peters children. Soon the young boy proudly called himself Cornelius Epp, not realizing of course that this exchange of names must have further saddened his mother. It was only much later, when the children had grown, that they returned to their original name and identity. Of the four children, only the two youngest daughters, Lena and Tina, were eventually returned to their mother—and only after much agitation on the part of Anna.

However well intentioned they were, the Russian Mennonites toward the end of the nineteenth century and the beginning of the twentieth often failed miserably to portray and practice the compassion and love of the Jesus they professed to follow. Cornelius C. Peters writes that the well-to-do farmers were considered by Mennonite society as especially blessed by God, whereas the poor were seen as those whom God had punished because they were lazy.

"We [Mennonites] did not learn," he writes, "that one should consider and help the poor. Instead everyone lived for himself only. Christianity meant attending church on Sundays, to sing hymns and pray, perhaps even to cry, and throughout the week the poor Russian workers were mistreated and beaten. . . . The food that was given to Russian workers often consisted of mere sour milk and bread. That was the Christianity we saw around us." Peters adds, "In the great Russian revolution (1917 to 1920), the Russians took terrible revenge on such Christianity."

During the Communist Revolution of 1917 the unmolested Mennonite world in Russia came to an end. In the 1920s many Mennonites left their homeland in search of a new existence elsewhere. The Peters, including Anna, and many others emigrated to Canada where they started a new life.

From 1929 to the end of her life in 1953, Anna Peters lived in Herbert, Saskatchewan. According to her obituary, written by her grandson Frank C. Peters, Anna belonged for most of her life to the Mennonite Brethren Church. "She loved the church," Peters wrote, "and sought to help with her 'widow's mite' wherever possible." When she died at age eighty-nine, Anna was quite ready to leave her sorrow-filled and burdensome life. As Peters reported, "Toward the end of her life, she talked often about having no desire for earthly things. She longed for the things that are above. God has answered her prayer."

In a cemetery just outside Herbert, Saskatchewan, Anna Peters found her final resting place.

35

Our Russian Maid

*H*elene Janzen of Winnipeg, Manitoba, tells this story: My parental home in South Russia lies far back in the past. Only in memory do I still relive from time to time our long house, its adjoining barn, and the beautiful garden in the back. I still see the mighty oak trees and blooming acacias, and above all, the stately chestnut tree. If the bench in the garden could speak, it would tell many stories, stories of love, longing, happiness—but also of disappointments and losses. I remember my father and mother, brothers and sisters—and I remember our Maria.

One autumn day Maria stood outside our door and asked for employment. She was tall, strongly built, a bit pale, with her hair combed tightly back around her head. She was not what people might call beautiful, but there was something attractive about her whole bearing. Perhaps it was her gray-blue eyes. They were not large nor had she long eyelashes, but her eyes shone with a brilliance all their own, adding a unique beauty to her open and trusting face. My parents took Maria into the house, and she became God's gift to us.

Maria was twenty-nine when she came, and she could neither read nor write. No girl in the village she came from had ever attended school. We children were eager to teach her. Karin, my younger sister, and I had some experience teaching illiterate people. Our little brother's nurse, Mokrina, had learned from us how to read and write, both Russian and German. Our teacher, who agreed kindly to read and correct Mokrina's work, placed a red five under the assignment, which meant "very good."

Now it was Maria's turn. Her young ten- and twelve-year-old teachers displayed zeal and patience in teaching her, and Maria was eager to learn. Her cheeks glowed when she drew the letters of the alphabet or spelled words. "O, my silly old head," she would say, laughing when she found her assignment difficult. But already in the second winter, she took her Russian New Testament—a Christmas gift from my parents—and tried to read in it.

During the long Russian winter evenings, when there was deep snow outside, or when the storm raged and the shutters rattled, the whole family sat around the long table with the comfortable hanging lamp over it. Maria would join us. Father either read or carved something, Mother knitted socks, we children did our homework, and Maria spelled and pronounced words from her Bible. From time to time she would turn to Father and ask, "*Nu djadja, oblasnite poshalusta, tshto eto snatshit?*" (Uncle, explain for me, please, what this means?). And my father would explain what was strange and new to her.

Maria was also present during our morning devotions around the breakfast table, without understanding much. But when Maria lifted her hand to cross herself, or when the simple cross she was wearing around her neck became visible, we felt a certain respect, even awe, in the presence of a deep faith which was foreign to us.

Then came the difficult years. All Russian servants had to be released. But Maria stayed with us. Her home, a small village north of Tshernigoff, was far away, and our home had become her home as well. When the anarchists came to our house and asked for Father, or when Makhno (an infamous oppressor) men came at night and demanded money and valuables, Maria was there and stood at Father's side. The good word of a maid in favor of her employer carried much weight among the common people, peasants, and workers.

Of course, against theft and plunder even Maria could do nothing, but at least Father was not beaten or tortured, and he remained alive—until October 30, 1919. On that day, before daybreak, Maria had to leave our village. A little bundle under her arm, she left our house, weeping. All Russian servants had to leave our village that day. After two days Maria returned, but my father was dead. It happened on a bright sunny day in late fall. Maria mourned Father's death with us.

We had become poor overnight and could no longer pay the wages of a maid. Mother told Maria that she would have to leave. But the faithful woman said, "I'll stay with you without pay!" And she stayed. She was now a real part of our family. She was proud when we children did well in school. When my oldest brother needed a suit, Maria insisted that Mother take the coarse linen cloth she had saved and sew clothes for the young man. Reluctantly Mother accepted the offer. The day before Pentecost we decorated, under Maria's supervision, our summer kitchen and hall with green branches. Maria herself covered the floors of these rooms with fresh-smelling grass she had cut for this purpose. That was the Russian custom.

Maria also stood side by side with Mother when we children were sick and needed extra care, and when our five-year-old brother died. Maria knew how to comfort us! At my brother's funeral, Maria made a beautiful wreath of autumn leaves, with red and white mums in it. She laid it on the little grave next to where Father had been buried the year before.

One day Maria experienced her great love. The Soviet government, after revolution, anarchy, and civil war, became more stable. Our village had to take in and quarter soldiers of the Red Army after it had defeated the White Army which had sought to reestablish the tsarist regime. Our earlier fears about the "Reds" now turned to pleasant surprise. These soldiers behaved in an orderly fashion, and many were polite, cultured, and educated.

We discovered that these military men had been followers of General Denikin of the White Army, with most of them having been officers. In the end they had surrendered to the Red Army. Among them was a young soldier, Kyrill, who caught the eye of our Maria. One day we children discovered Maria and Kyrill sitting side by side on a hidden bench in the garden. They held hands and spoke softly.

After that Maria's eyes sparkled more than usual. During her work around the house, she smiled and hummed tunes. She also seemed more tender toward us children, pressing us more closely to herself before bedtime. Soon the military left again. Sometime later we saw Maria sitting alone on the garden bench, reading a letter and in her left hand holding a small photo of the man she loved. After that she never heard from Kyrill again. The sparkle in her eyes diminished, and she became sad and even moody at times.

Before long Maria expressed the wish to see her home village again. She seemed to feel she was no longer needed in our home. My aunt, who had come to live with us, once said to my mother, "Anna, you allow Maria too much freedom. She has come to think that *she* is the mistress of this house!"

Perhaps there was some truth to that, but I don't know any more what my good mother's answer was. Thus Maria prepared to leave. The cow we had given her as a gift was sold, and my mother gave her blankets, towels, and bedsheets. Maria hugged and kissed us all, wept, and drove away.

A few years later Maria came to visit us. Sitting with all of us around the family table, she told us about her life since she had left. Her eyes sparkled as never before, and her cheeks glowed with excitement. She had been elected as the only woman to the village council. "No other woman in the village," she said with a twinkle in her eye, "could read or write!" She was about to become a Soviet activist, which was an honor and made her happy. Thus Maria shared her joy with us, not noticing that this change in her made us all sad.

Later that day I went with her into the garden to look for some last sweet plums. It was an autumn day, windy, and the clouds raced across the sky. I couldn't help but tell her my secret—I was in love and I told her the name of the man.

"Well, well," she said, "Vladimir Henrychovich, your one-time teacher! How happy I am for you! He was a good man. He was a truly educated man and yet always polite toward me, a simple Russian maid, just as polite and friendly as he was toward your aunt, the daughter of a rich estate owner."

I knew Maria would agree that I had made the right choice. Now that Maria knew about my love and intended marriage, I was doubly happy.

We never heard from Maria again. At first we received reports about her from people who had been to her village. The rest of the information about her was supplied by my imagination. She lives now, I believe, in a small, white-washed house, built for her with assistance from the village council. She lives a quiet and withdrawn life. In the past she had achieved the pinnacle of her success, but today they don't need her anymore. Her neighbors' girls read and write fluently, they talk intelligently about algebra and trigonometry, things about which Maria knows nothing. Today the schoolyard of her village is alive with blond and brown-haired girls and boys. The son of her brother even studies in Moscow.

Maria's pleasures are simple ones. She milks her cow in the warm barn and feeds her few chickens. In spring she plants potatoes and cabbage, and in summer she delights in her climbing roses along the walls of her house and in the golden sunflowers in the backyard. In fall she cuts the heavy sunflower discs and puts them on the flat roof of the barn to dry. Later she knocks out the sunflower seeds with a stick, winnows them on a windy day, and puts them into a sack. In winter, during the long Russian evenings when the neighbor lady comes over for a chat, Maria smilingly offers her a handful of roasted sunflower seeds.

I wonder if Maria has an icon hanging in the corner of her room. Is our family picture among her other photographs on the wall? And her Russian New Testament—does she still read it and pray in the evening? I know she has not become a bitter woman. I also know that Maria did not just serve a Mennonite family. She gave of herself, sharing her rich life with all of us.

Sometimes Maria no doubt thinks of my father, my mother, and us brothers and sisters. She remembers our parental home—the long house, the mighty oak trees, and the blooming acacias. In her memory she visits our garden with its chestnut tree and the bench. She looks for us but does not find us there. She doesn't know that a large part of our family was exiled to Siberia and some have died. Some made it to faraway Canada. It is just as well Maria doesn't know any of this. May God reward her for what she was to us.

36

Whose Land?

*I*n the summer of 1873, twelve Russian Mennonite deputies came to Manitoba to investigate settlement possibilities. They did not fully realize that the natives of that province, including Indians and Métis, worried about losing their land and their traditional rights and claims to newcomers from Europe. Just a few years before, in 1870, the rebellion at Red River led by Louis Riel had made it abundantly clear to the Canadian government that the natives and their rights had to be taken seriously. And while the Mennonite settlers later developed good relations with the Indians and Métis of Manitoba, there were at the beginning considerable tensions between the two peoples, cultures, and traditions. Here is a dramatic example of such tensions.

* * *

On June 17, 1873, twelve delegates from Russia, led by William Hespeler, a Canadian government official, docked at Winnipeg. They were welcomed by the officials, including the governor, who sought to impress the Mennonites with his province and the opportunities in it. Winnipeg at the time had fewer than 3,000 inhabitants, and the total for the province was not much over 15,000. Of this number all but about 2,000 whites were Indians or people of mixed blood called Métis. But there was, of course, much open and fertile land, and the Canadian government sought to settle the vast western prairies with farmers from European countries.

After inspecting the soil conditions in southern Manitoba, some delegates had seen enough and proceeded south to the United States. However, five of the delegates and William Hespeler traveled west of Winnipeg all the way to the foot of the Riding Mountains. On their way back to Winnipeg, they were met by a number of Métis, whose behavior frightened the Mennonites and caused Hespeler to fear for all their lives. The incident was described in detail by the province's paper, *The Manitoban*, in its July 5, 1873, issue.

The Mennonite party had arrived about halfway between Poplar Point and House's Tavern, about twenty-five wiles west of Winnipeg, when the horse and wagon caravan was overtaken by a French Métis on horseback. It was Dominion Day, a national holiday, and the rider, named McKay, had possibly had too much to drink. McKay approached the lead wagon which contained Hespeler himself. McKay challenged the driver, George Rath (not a Mennonite), to a race and gave one wagon horse a lash with his whip. George Rath in turn struck at McKay's horse. Growing more angry, McKay again struck Rath's horses. Rath lashed back, hitting not only the rider's horse but also the rider, knocking off his cap.

McKay picked up his cap, turned, and rode home. On the way he met two friends, Jackson and Desjairais. He told them what happened and that he was going to get a gun and kill the driver who had struck him. When McKay returned with a gun and was about to pursue the caravan, his friends realized the man was serious and needed to be stopped. They jumped off their carts, snatched the gun from him and broke it.

McKay, however, would not be dissuaded. He overtook the Mennonite party at House's Tavern where they had stopped to water and feed the animals. He again threatened to kill the driver who had struck him, and he abused the others with foul language. Exasperated at McKay's abusive language, another driver, not Rath, knocked McKay off his horse.

Before long other Métis came to the assistance of McKay. Together they attacked the Mennonite group, driving all of them into the house. McKay rode off to get yet more help and returned with two mounted companions armed with guns. Again Jackson and Desjairais, together with other peaceable people, took their guns away. But McKay, still not pacified, rode off toward Poplar Point to get even more assistance. Soon about ten more men appeared, all vowing they would take revenge on the foreign delegation.

William Hespeler now realized that the situation was very serious. He dispatched the following message to Lieutenant-Governor Alexander Morris: "We are attacked by Halfe Breeds. . . . We are in danger of our lives . . . please send soldiers at once as we cannot leave the place."

In the meantime the delegates had gone upstairs, defending the staircase as well as they could. They ultimately retreated to a room and locked the door. Hespeler, revolver in hand, placed himself at the door to guard it. He assured the Mennonites that he would protect and defend them—with his life if necessary. Later Hespeler was asked whether he would have killed the attackers. "Yes, I would have killed them had they broken down the door," he said. "I have my children and myself to live for, and I am committed to the government to be your protector on this tour."

Fortunately, there was no bloodshed in the incident. The lieutenant-governor dispatched some fifty troops to House's Tavern, and at half-past five the next morning, the prisoners were released. McKay, three of his brothers, and a brother-in-law, all of whom had played prominent roles in the disturbance, were arrested and brought to Winnipeg for trial.

As could be expected, the opinions of the news media about the incident varied. The *Manitoba Free Press* stated in its July 5 issue that "it seems more than likely that directly the affair may be attributed to a recklessness begotten of drunkenness." However, the French-language paper, *Le Métis*, insisted that the driver of the Mennonite wagon had struck McKay first and that when the Métis had come to House's Tavern, another driver had struck McKay with a revolver, cutting him above the eye.

Whatever the truth concerning the details in this incident, the situation was no doubt a result of the Métis' anxieties. They feared they would be displaced by the immigrants. They were apprehensive about the government's determination to establish political control over them without regard for their wishes, culture, and participation. As Alexander Morris recorded for his own file, "Some of the Half Breeds no doubt view with displeasure the large immigration which is coming into the Province."

Those Mennonite deputies who decided to recommend settlement in Manitoba were grateful to the Canadian authorities for the prompt action and protection they received in the incident at House's Tavern. They went to Ottawa where they signed an agreement to begin a major immigration to Canada the following year. Between 1874 and 1880 some seven thousand Russian Mennonites settled in Manitoba. The confrontation with the Métis had no adverse affect on the immigration movement, except perhaps that the Mennonites decided not to settle near the Riding Mountains. They instead located themselves closer to where there would be protection in case of trouble.

The confrontation between the Mennonites and the Métis in 1873 gives rise to some thoughts about the Mennonites' knowledge of and attitude toward the natives of Manitoba and the relationship between these two peoples.

Jacob Y. Shantz, a Mennonite businessman of Berlin (Kitchener), Ontario, did much to help settle the Russian Mennonites in Manitoba. He assured the Canadian government, among other things, that the Mennonites would be good neighbors to the native population.

Some had warned Shantz about settling Mennonites in the West: "Are you not afraid," they asked, "to be among these half-breeds without any weapons of self-defense?"

Shantz had replied, "No, therein lies my safety; [the natives] know that my purpose is a good one, and since I have no weapons, they become my protectors, and I eat and sleep with them without fear of being molested." In a report to the government about his first trip West, Shantz had stated, "[The aborigines] are a civilized class of people. I have been amongst them as a stranger, have boarded and lodged with them, and have invariably found them very obliging and hospitable."

When asked why then these people had rebelled against the government in 1870, Shantz explained, "They thought that our Government should first consult them and give them a certain right to the lands they then occupied, and also lands for their children."

Shantz was convinced that the natives of Manitoba were a peace-

ful people. "They are quiet and inoffensive," he wrote. "The Indians who once enter into a treaty will keep it to the letter, but when a promise to them is broken, they are not only dissatisfied, but will assuredly seek revenge."

Shantz accompanied the Russian-Mennonite deputies to Manitoba in 1873, together with John F. Funk, a U.S. Mennonite minister and editor of the widely read Mennonite periodical *Herald of Truth*. Commenting on the relationship between the Métis and white settlers, Funk wrote, "Bad white men have taught them bad principles and have awakened in them the deep spirit of revenge. . . . They too judge the tree by its fruits, and because there are many bad Christians, it is hard to make them believe that there are any good ones."

There were, however, also those among the Mennonite deputies who were less positive about the natives of Manitoba. Paul Tschetter of the Hutterian Brethren wrote in his diary, "The people are lazy farmers of mixed Indian blood and are more cattlemen than agriculturists." He added, "The half-breed Indians live on this land, and it belongs to them."

Another deputy, Wilhelm Ewert of Prussia, shared Tschetter's sentiments. He did not like the country he saw and did not think that his people should settle in Manitoba. The natives only increased his "antipathy toward this place." He complained about the drunkenness of the Métis and added, "The Indians . . . are not attractive neighbors. Although otherwise harmless, there is no limit to an Indian's thirst for revenge if he feels cheated somehow. Several times they have already rebelled against the government, and while the latest [1870] was ineffectual, they have been promised things which it is doubtful that they can be kept."

The attitude of Tschetter and Ewert toward the natives of Manitoba did not represent that of the other deputies who decided to settle along the Red River. The newcomers found that the Indians and Métis were helpful; the relationship which developed between the two peoples were cordial. Already the deputies, including Ewert and Tobias Unruh, had enjoyed the goodwill and hospitality of Indians.

Unruh wrote, "They gave us a good supper. After supper we sang a hymn and prayed, then went to bed." Tschetter too was impressed with the home of one of the "half-breed Indians." He wrote, "His wife and servants treated us very nicely. He had a beautiful house, his floor covered with rugs. . . . The housewife gave us a good supper, for they are wealthy people."

The Russian Mennonites came to a land which belonged to Canada's natives, a fact partly recognized by the first Mennonite settlers in Manitoba. As a result of Canada's policy of settling the West, the Indian and Métis people were displaced by the newcomers and relegated to reservations and an existence of poverty and dependence on the dominant white society. Being generally peaceful and friendly toward new immigrants, the natives were also understandably worried about their land and future existence. Mennonites owe much to the Manitoba natives. Without the goodwill and assistance of Indians and Métis, the Mennonites' beginning in Manitoba would have been much more difficult.

37

A Blizzard Baby

*D*r. Grace Kaiser practiced medicine in New Holland, a town in eastern Lancaster County, Pennsylvania, for twenty-eight years. Spending much of her time as a "baby doctor" among the Old Order Amish and Mennonite people of the area, she was respected and loved by her patients and their relatives. "Dr. Frau," as she was affectionately called, became disabled in 1978 and had to give up her practice. She now devotes much of her time to writing books dealing with her interesting experiences as a medical doctor among the Mennonites and Amish. The following story has been adapted from a chapter in one of her books, *Dr. Frau*.

* * *

The storm, according to reports, originated in the Gulf of Mexico, then moved northeast as a blizzard. It bore across Georgia, the Carolinas, and into Virginia. There was no doubt that Lancaster County would experience the full brunt of the blizzard.

People in the New Holland area hurried to prepare for what was to come. Farmers hauled extra fodder from fields into barns; women made quick trips to grocery stores; and trucks, cars, and buggies rushed on last-minute errands, congesting the roads and highways.

Dr. Kaiser also prepared for the storm. After lunch she delivered a pre-storm baby, glad for one less birth to worry about during a blizzard. She hurried through the countryside finishing rounds to patients who might be isolated for several days.

As she was driving home in her station wagon late in the afternoon, the first snowflakes began to fall. Before long the wind picked up and the snow fell heavily, covering fence posts, bushes, and the road with its whiteness. Visibility was greatly reduced, and with the heavy snow on the slippery road, the doctor had to drive slowly.

When she finally arrived home, the doctor's housekeeper was about to leave the house. "Looks like the real thing out there," the housekeeper said without her usual smile. "I better go buy bread and milk if there's any left."

Shortly after supper the telephone rang. "This is Martin Weaver," the voice at the other end said. "Guess you better come out. We think Martha's in labor."

"How are your roads?" the doctor asked.

"Ours is drifted shut but Shirk Road is still open," Martin said. "I'll meet you at the corner in half an hour with the carriage and drive ya in."

"Okay, I'll start out now," the doctor said without enthusiasm. Replacing the receiver she turned to her husband, Peter, and said, "Lucky you!"

Dr. Kaiser telephoned Anna, her assistant, who often accompanied her on home deliveries. She put on heavy clothes, threw a shovel into the station wagon, and backed out the driveway. Down the block she stopped at Anna's house and blew the horn.

"What a night," Anna said as she got into the wagon and shut the door. "Think we'll have to walk tonight?"

"We'll see," the doctor said as she started to drive into the raging storm. Outside New Holland, unprotected by houses, snow drifts were already rising and made driving difficult. Eventually they reached Shirk Road. The doctor recalled this same road in springtime when violets, wild mustard, and dandelion covers the banks and the air is perfumed with honeysuckle. But there was little time for such reverie. The doctor had to concentrate on the road now. On the crest of a hill, she stopped the station wagon. The headlights shone across a valley of shifting snow, rapidly filling the road between steep banks.

"This is as far as we can drive," the doctor said to Anna. "Less than a mile to meet Martin."

"We can't walk through that mess," Anna objected. "They wouldn't find our bodies for a week."

"There's only one other possibility," the doctor said as she nodded toward the outlines of a small house near the road. "A young Mennonite couple live here. We'll ask William to help us. His wife is due in March. He'll understand."

Fighting the wind and blowing snow, the doctor reached the house. She removed a glove and pounded the outer door as hard as she could. "William! William! Wake up! I need help. William Burkholder, wake up!" she shouted repeatedly.

At last William got up, lighted a lamp, and came to the door. "What are you doing out tonight, Dr. Frau?" William asked as he rubbed his sleepy eyes.

"Can you hitch up and take Anna and me to meet Martin Weaver at the next crossroad? It's baby time for them."

"Yes, of course," William said, "but all we have is a small buggy with one seat. We're just married, you know."

Before long William came with his horse and buggy, helped the two women into the seat, and sat beside the doctor who had to hold Anna on her lap. He spread a blanket over all three of them.

"Up, Sue. Giddy up," William shouted, slapping the reins over the horse's back. "Hope the snow doesn't get too deep. Sometimes horses lie down in deep drifts."

Pulling hard, the horse did not let the occupants of the buggy down. It seemed much longer, but it could not have taken more than twenty minutes to drive the half mile to where Martin was waiting. He appeared like a black speck in a sea of white.

"Hi, Kaiser. Good to see ya. There's no hurry," Martin shouted above the howling wind. "The missus thinks she'll have it tonight. Better to get ya in plenty a time."

Martin slid open the side door of his carriage, set the doctor's bag inside, and told the women to get in. As he waited for his passengers to be seated, he held his wide-brimmed hat with both hands. Getting inside the carriage he said, "It'll be rough riding tonight. Road's closed. We'll have to go through the fields." He spat a dark spurt into the snow and shifted the chewing tobacco in his cheek.

The Weavers were an older, established Mennonite family and owned a closed carriage. But the vehicle was built for transportation, not comfort. It had leaf-springs, but driving across the frozen and snowy field of corn rows separated by deep valleys, into which the wheels kept falling with a thud, was no joy ride. Except for the howling blizzard outside, the only noise was the wagon bouncing over the corrugated field. The women felt pain in all their joints.

At last they reached the Weaver farm. Martin helped the women from the carriage and through a hip-high drift encircling the house. They struggled into the kitchen, dimly lit by a small lamp on a long table, and took off their heavy overcoats and boots.

"Hello there! What a night to bring you out," Martha called through the open bedroom door. "Guess I'll have this baby sometime tonight."

"We certainly hope so after that trip," the doctor answered as she continued to peel off her heavy clothing. "Babies have no respect for bad weather."

The doctor walked stocking-footed through the kitchen and bedroom over a cold linoleum floor. A portable heater gave off some warmth in the sleeping room but also kerosene odors. Martha's gray hair and placid face showed above the quilts. She was about thirty-six, had given birth to seven children, and had had four miscarriages. A pale kerosene lamp accented the furrows around her sagging chin and sad brown eyes.

The doctor unpacked her bag and examined the woman. "Sometime tonight," the doctor said as she covered Martha.

"I'll be glad to have it over," Martha said quietly, turning her face toward the wall. "The children will be happy for a new baby." Turning to the two women, Martha added, "Make yourself comfortable in the kitchen."

When Martin came in from the barn, he asked the two women in the kitchen whether they were cold. His smile showed brown irregular teeth. Some were missing, which added to his old appearance. "I'll make it warmer in here," he said and picked out a few sticks and dropped them into the fire box. He then removed his workshoes, lay down beside Martha, covered himself with other blankets, and soon snored loudly.

The doctor and Anna tried to keep warm as well as they could.

They fed the fire through most of the night with wood stored under the steps. They listened to the storm outside, catnapped, and occasionally left their chairs to walk around the kitchen. At five in the morning the doctor went to check Martha. Martha had begun to moan. Her moans grew louder. Doctor Kaiser knew she had not come in vain.

"Ugh, ugh. It's soon here," Martha grunted at seven o'clock.

Martin got up and rushed to turn up the bedroom heater. He went to get another heater from the washhouse and piled wood into the kitchen stove. Warm air began to fill the rooms.

Upstairs the children were moving. Not wanting the children's presence during the birth, Martin shouted up the staircase in Pennsylvania German, ordering them to stay in their bedrooms. There were no objections nor questions. His word was law.

Seating himself on a chair near the bed, Martin said to Martha, "Lie still. Push hard. It's soon over." The doctor and Anna were occupied with the birth of the baby.

As dawn's first glimmer shone in the east through the kitchen windows, a writhing baby girl lay on the bed.

"We could have used another boy around here," Martin said half in jest.

"Girls are better than boys," the doctor teased. "They work in the house *and* barn."

Martin laughed and said, "But girls don't haul manure." He added, "Maybe we'll have a boy next time."

Martha seemed to ignore her husband's remark. Turning to Anna, who was dressing the baby, she said, "I'm glad it's over. I was worried about being snowed in."

Dr. Kaiser marveled at how much younger Martha suddenly seemed. She glowed in the triumph of a new birth as she hugged the new baby. "I can't wait for the children to see their new sister," she said. "The last baby is three already."

Martin lifted the green window shades. The morning sun made the snow glare. Across the landscape shadowed drifts rose and fell. The storm was finished. Windless trees stood mute beside the house.

Alta, a sixteen-year-old daughter, came to care for her mother and prepare breakfast for the family. Martin prepared to take the doctor and Anna back to their vehicle. They then followed the tracks along the banks of Shirk Road, tracks made by other travelers that morning. The doctor wondered how many days would pass before plows cleared the snow drifts from back roads.

It was William who again helped the women get the station wagon going. Because of the snow under the hood it refused to start. It had to be towed to the New Holland Pike. Finally the engine turned over and the two women sputtered home.

By mid-morning Dr. Kaiser sat in her warm kitchen and wearily removed her boots. Her husband, Peter, walked past her, humming a cheerful tune. He carried a snow shovel and gave instructions to two of their children who were in snowsuits to face the after-blizzard new day.

"Have a good night, dear?" he asked his wife.

38

The Spear of the Moros

*F*rom the time the Mennonites first settled in the Paraguayan Chaco, the Lengua Indians warned them against possible attacks from a warlike tribe living farther north. Knowing little about the Ayoreo or Moro Indians, the Mennonites did not take the warnings seriously. In 1935 the Mennonites established a mission to the Indians of the Chaco. This "Light to the Indians" mission included efforts to establish contact with the Moros as well.

Through Moros themselves and missionaries from the New Tribes Mission and the Catholic Church, the Mennonites gradually came to know the Moros. They learned that the Moros subsisted at the edge of the bush north of the Mennonite settlements by fishing, hunting, and some agriculture. Their weapons were spears, bows, and arrows. They respected men with weapons. Thus even missionaries working among them had to carry weapons. For fear that the spirit of a slain enemy resided in the blood, they discarded any blood-stained spears. They generally did not take prisoners, but sometimes captured women and children and made these captives work for them. They gladly accepted gifts—but disliked mirrors, believing they personified higher powers.

The coming of the settlers to the Gran Chaco and the war between Paraguay and Bolivia in 1932-1935 pushed the Moros deeper into the bush. Beginning in 1947 they began attacking outlying settlements. They killed and wounded several Mennonites and other settlers. When in the 1950s the North American Pure Oil Company began to build roads and drill for oil in Moro territory, the attacks on settlements and oil company establishments increased.

Having tried for years to contact the Moros, the Mennonite mission committee decided in 1958 that the time for advancing into the tribe's territory had come. They believed the oil company's bases close to the Moros, as well as good relations between the Mennonites and the oil men, would benefit the missionary project.

Two experienced missionaries were chosen for the undertaking. One was David Hein, married with six children. The other was Kornelius Isaak, also married and with three children. The missionaries, who spoke Spanish but not the Moro language, were eager to go even though they knew the dangers. A Lengua Indian was to accompany them.

In August 1958, the three missionaries started out with a Jeep and trailer on the 173-kilometer journey north to where the oil company had its camp. From there they penetrated some fifty kilometers into the thick bush. They could drive only slowly, for the roads were narrow and swampy. Several times they had to dig out their vehicle from the mud. At last they came to a shallow body of water in which fish were found.

Suddenly the Indian said, "There's fire nearby."

Hein and Isaak had not smelled or noticed anything. Leaving the Jeep, the missionaries discovered footprints on the ground and a few fires burning here and there. They stuck sticks in the ground, attached shirts to them, and returned to camp.

The next day the three missionaries drove out again to the spot they had visited. They found that the shirts had been removed and parrot feathers were attached to the sticks. They interpreted this as a positive sign. Taking the feathers as a gift from the Moros, they fastened additional shirts to the sticks and left again.

When they returned the following day, the missionaries found additional signs. There were three sticks with parrot feathers on two of them and one had vulture feathers attached to it. Beneath the sticks were an empty wooden bowl and a bag. The sticks, they found to their amazement, were partly debarked and painted redbrown.

The Lengua Indian felt uneasy about these signs. Later he explained that the empty bowl and bag might mean that the Moros were poor and nothing could be gotten from them. The red-brown sticks might mean a declaration of war and bloodshed.

The missionaries drove home to Filadelfia to report what they had found and to confer with the mission committee and their families. The mission committee counseled caution. The committee members said that, in view of the ominous signs and danger, they were not prepared to send the missionaries to the Moros. If they decided to go on their own, however, the committee would support and stand behind them and their undertaking.

The families of Hein and Isaak were fearful for the two men, but in the end they let them go. They believed this might be the first step toward bringing the gospel to the Moros. The missionaries themselves, while concerned about their safety, were eager to continue their mission, come what might.

On September 10, 1958, the two missionaries and another Lengua Indian started out from the oil company's camp. They had driven only a few kilometers into Moro territory when the Indian guide said, "There they are!"

Ahead was a group of some fifty men scantily clad and apparently without weapons. The missionaries stopped their Jeep, got off, and waved to the natives. The men seemed friendly, came closer, and accepted gifts from the missionaries. A tall Indian approached Kornelius. Looking over the Indian's shoulder, Kornelius noticed that Indians farther back were carrying weapons. Things did not bode well.

What happened next was sudden. The men shouted insolent words at the missionaries and demanded more gifts. Then one tried to wrestle the Lengua Indian to the ground. The Lengua sought to grab the hunting rifle in the Jeep but was unable to reach it. David Hein, seeing his native friend in trouble, took hold of the rifle and waved it high in the air. When the Moros saw this they retreated, but not before one of them had pointed an arrow at David. He did not release the bow, however.

While all this was going on, Kornelius Isaak felt an intense pain. In the next moment he pulled out a thin spear from his side. No one had seen how it all had happened. From all appearances the wound did not seem that serious. Turning the Jeep around, Kornelius at the wheel urged that they return to the camp as quickly as possible. But after driving only a short distance, Kornelius became so weak David had to continue driving.

At the oil company camp, Kornelius was taken by airplane to Filadelfia and admitted to the hospital. The doctors found that his spleen and kidneys were badly damaged; he required an operation. The next day, with his wife, Marg, his parents, and many friends at his side, Kornelius died. His last words were a prayer for the Moro Indians whom he had tried to reach.

The New Tribes Mission and Catholic missionaries continued to work among the Moros. The tribe became more open to the whites and eventually individuals accepted the Christian gospel. In 1961 Mennonites learned why the Moros had attacked the three missionaries. When the oil company had made contact with the Moros, an epidemic among them had broken out in which three of their people had died. This made them very angry at the whites. When the missionaries pushed into their area, they stabbed Isaak in revenge.

The Moros learned the missionary had died of the wound. Then an even worse epidemic broke out among them, in which four more of their people died. They now believed they were being punished for killing Isaak. According to missionary Bill Pencille, who related this story, the Moros promised not to be as hostile toward the settlers anymore.

Eventually a number of the Moro Indians were baptized. Some came to the Mennonite settlements seeking employment and other material benefits. In 1988, thirty years after the tragic death of a Mennonite missionary, a group of Moros came to the Fernheim Colony for a visit. Among the group were men who had been part of the warrior band that attacked the missionaries.

On this festive occasion several photos were taken. One picture includes David Hein and Sidabi with his family. Sidabi is the man who in 1958 aimed an arrow at Hein. In another picture Marg, Kornelius Isaak's widow, and her grown children stand with Jonoine, an Indian, between them. Jonoine holds the spear with which he had killed the family's husband and father.

Former enemies had become brothers and sisters.

39

Shot Down over Germany

During World War II many Canadian and U.S. Mennonites refused to serve in the military. They chose instead to work in alternative programs provided by their governments. The story of these conscientious objectors (COs) has been told in numerous Mennonite publications. These Cos have been models for other young people faced with the draft.

Not so well known is the fact that just as many Mennonite young men served their country in the armed forces during World War II. Some died on the battlefields, while others came home to tell their story, even though their home communities were not always willing to listen. Henry Pankratz was one young Mennonite man who joined the Canadian Air Force and survived to tell his story.

Henry was the son of William and Maria Pankratz, who emigrated to Canada in 1923. The Pankratzs had experienced the Communist Revolution of 1917, the collapse of Mennonite institutional life during World War I, and the loss of their Russian homeland in a time of chaos, anarchy, and terror. They were thus happy to find a new home near Langham, Saskatchewan. One of Henry's brothers, Bill, joined the air force in 1941. Henry decided to join the air force as well, serving eventually as a radio officer in the Canadian bomber squadron.

On December 6, 1944, Henry's crew took off from England on their sixth bombing raid over Germany. "The trip there was uneventful," Henry later wrote, obviously not thinking about the destruction of property and loss of life their raid must have caused. Having accomplished their mission, they were homeward bound when a German fighter plane attacked. Their plane caught fire, and the pilot gave the order to jump. Henry was the third man to get out. His parachute opened inside the plane, which by now was badly out of control. Fortunately the chute did not get tangled.

Henry writes, "I hung in the air, stationary it seemed, for a long time. Falling not far from me was a big ball of fire. It was the aircraft I had just vacated. A moment later it blew up and went hurtling to the ground. I thought I'd never reach the good earth. The darkness was so intense I could hardly see the chute above me.

"Suddenly I felt a terrific impact, as though a truck had hit me. I realized I was on the ground. I was dragged about ten yards before I managed to free myself from the harness and collapse the chute."

Since it was raining hard, Henry sought shelter in a nearby clump of trees, wrapped the parachute around himself, and lay quiet. Through the trees he saw a faint glimmer of light and heard dogs barking. Soon he heard voices close by and someone with a flashlight passed. It must have been a farmer who had seen the airplane go down and was looking for survivors. Henry, afraid of being discovered, remained perfectly still.

Henry was puzzled by distant gunfire until it occurred to him it must be the ammunition exploding in the wrecked aircraft. He had a fair idea of where he was, for the navigator had told the pilot just before they were hit that they were nearing the German-Dutch border. But Henry did not know the time. He had lost his wristwatch when he jumped. As he waited for morning before doing anything else, he was caught in a cold, penetrating December rain.

In the early dawn of the morning, Henry recognized the faint outlines of a farm house a quarter of a mile away. He hid his parachute and Mae West (an inflatable life jacket) among the bushes and began walking toward the farm. The house and barn were all one building, typical of the farms in northwest Germany. Finding the barn door locked, he sat outside and waited. Sometime later he heard noises and voices in the barn. Peering through a crack in the door, he saw a woman and a man, both wearing wooden shoes, doing morning chores. A lantern was their only light.

After Henry's repeated knocking on the barn door, the man came to the door, obviously surprised to see a stranger. The downed airman was invited to come in the house, offered a chair, and asked many questions. The German family was amazed at how well Henry spoke German, marveled at his fine uniform, and commented on how well he looked after his ordeal. He was advised to take off his flying boots, which a young girl put in the oven. The family gave him coffee to drink and black bread to eat, food Henry did not find very tasty. They continued to chat like friends, with the Germans showing Henry photographs of their son, a prisoner of war in England. The Germans were disgusted with the war, hoping it would soon be over.

At first the family, whose name Henry has forgotten, wanted to hide Henry from the German authorities. But in the end they decided against it because there was a strange woman living with them who could not be trusted to keep the secret. The family assured Henry that as a prisoner of war he would be treated well and after the war could go home.

Henry was taken by his German captor to the nearby town of Uelsen, where he was handed over to the police and interrogated. He was then taken to another town and locked in a prison cell. As he was led along the way, people jeered him. In prison Henry met two of his crew who had also been captured. Three other crew members had died in the crash, the prisoners learned later.

For the next several months, the prisoners of war were transported from prison to prison and camp to camp, interrogated repeatedly, and treated according to the moods of the guards and other officials. In one camp the prisoners had to take off their clothes for searches while male and female personnel looked on.

Traveling by train and on foot, Henry saw what Allied bombing had done to German cities. In Hanover, for example, he saw flames and smoke in parts of the city caused by bombs the Allies had dropped the night before. German civilians who met the POWs in the streets expressed anger and hostility toward them. The guards did all they could to protect the prisoners from the people.

When the war ended with Germany's collapse in the spring of 1945, Henry found himself on the Soviet side, in what later became East Germany. On May 20 a convoy of Russian trucks drove Henry and other POWs to the American zone. Arriving in Halle in the evening, Henry ate his fill of good food, including white bread.

He later wrote, "Till then, I never realized white bread was so white." On May 25 Henry was flown to a Canadian ex-POW camp near Brussels and the following evening to Ford, England. "Never was a landing more welcome!" Henry writes in his characteristically laconic manner. Boarding a ship in England, he reached Halifax, Canada, on July 20, 1945. "The road back was completed."

When asked how he feels now about having served in the air force, Henry expresses no regrets. "I consider my air force experience to be the highlight of my life," he writes. "We didn't make much money, but we had a great life and made some wonderful friends. I wouldn't have missed it for anything. I still miss it."

He explains his decision to join the Canadian Air Force: "I and my brothers always felt that Canada gave our parents a new life and an opportunity to live in peace and harmony and raise a family in the best country in the world, and therefore worth fighting for. As a result we often found ourselves at variance with Mennonite tradition and/or religious beliefs. However, I take the position 'To each his own.' I have no quarrel with the [conscientious] objectors, but take a dim view at their judgmental attitude. So be it!"

After the war Henry joined the Royal Canadian Mounted Police for about two years. He resigned from the RCMP because he found life there too confining. Henry got married in Camrose, Alberta, then rejoined the air force. He served in peacetime until 1968 in such places as Goose Bay, Labrador, Montreal, West Germany, Manitoba, Alberta, Quebec—and finally Ontario, where he retired from the air force. After that he was employed by General Motors as a traveling auditor for thirteen years. Finally he worked on security for Ontario Hydro, where, he writes, "They made me retire when I reached age sixty-five."

Perhaps the question of military service will never be fully resolved among Mennonites. From the beginning of Anabaptist-Mennonite history, there have been sincere advocates of nonresistance and pacifism on the one hand, and sincere proponents of the view that it is a Christian's duty to defend the nation when called on.

There have been the Balthasar Hubmaiers and so-called sword-bearers among the Anabaptists and Mennonites, who served in the army and engaged in self-defense throughout the centuries. But there have also been the Michael Sattlers and peaceful Anabaptists and Mennonites who believed that the sword, while instituted by God for the protection of the good and punishment of the bad, is "outside the perfection of Christ."

Mennonites and other Christians should remember their heritage and learn from the teaching and example of the Prince of Peace to walk in Christ's ways. They should also respect those who in good conscience hold another position.

40

Hate and Love

*T*he apostle Paul had some un-flattering things to say about the people of Crete. Writing to young Titus, whom he had appointed pastor of the first Christian church on the island, Paul in Titus 1:12 quoted a Cretan prophet: "Cretans are always liars, evil beasts, lazy gluttons."

When Peter J. Dyck of Mennonite Central Committee (MCC) visited Bishop Irineos of Crete, the two men talked about these harsh words. The bishop said with a twinkle in his eyes, "Cretans may not be liars and certainly aren't beasts, but they always have been fighters." He added, "There's a violent streak in us. We Cretans are proud of being fighters."

Here, adapted from Peter Dyck's account, is a story that bears out the bishop's words, though with a twist at the end.

* * *

It happened during World War II. After Greece had been captured by the Germans, and a few days before the German military invaded the island of Crete, the Cretans were given an ultimatum: surrender or face destruction and death.

The Cretans didn't need much time to make up their minds. Their answer to the Germans was, "Oxi! No!"

On May 20, 1941, German airplanes darkened the sky over the island and countless parachutes descended on the hapless people.

Men, women, and even teenage children grabbed whatever was at hand—guns, pitchforks, axes—and killed German soldiers as they landed.

But the occupying forces were too strong; Crete fell to the Germans. Many Cretans fled into the mountains and other hideouts from where they waged guerrilla war against their enemies. Those freedom fighters who were caught by the German military were severely punished, often with death.

One day a German officer driving his Jeep near the village of Kandanos was shot and killed. The Germans demanded that the inhabitants of Kandanos reveal the identity of the killers. Of course, nobody would tell. So the Germans rounded up all men and boys thirteen years and older, lined them up, and shot them all dead. The military then came with bulldozers and destroyed all the buildings in the village, making the place a mere rubble heap. A few days later the Germans put up a plaque there as a warning. It read, "Here stood Kandanos. It was demolished because Cretans killed a German soldier."

Peter Dyck now knew why Cretans hated Germans. He had also heard them say more than once that the only good German was a dead German. Dyck was saddened by this, but there was more for him to learn about what happened during the war years.

Taking Dyck on a tour of his beautiful island, Bishop Irineos showed him the countryside, introduced him to the people, and brought him face-to-face with reminders of the war. Near Kandanos Dyck saw a pyramid of German soldiers' skulls. And at a monastery he saw an old building which contained hundreds, perhaps thousands, of coffins with the remains of German soldiers. Dyck shuddered at these sights.

The bishop said, "It's true we Cretans are fighters and hate the Germans." He added, "But we also love the church."

Dyck was still wondering at the bishop's sudden change of subject when the bishop said in a pleading tone of voice, "Will you do it? Please don't say no." Bishop Irineos was asking whether MCC could send young people to Crete to help the people rebuild their lives and economy.

"Soon Crete will be an island of old people," the bishop continued. "If you could just send us a few craftsmen to train our young people. With new skills they would find new jobs. Then they would stay here. Perhaps you could start a vocational training school."

Dyck promised to see what he could do, but both men realized it would be difficult to implement the bishop's plans. Cretans were not only proud and strong-willed people, they were also Orthodox Christians strongly tied to their tradition. For them the Bible and tradition were almost equally important. The men and women who volunteered to serve with MCC, on the other hand, were Christians who believed in peace and nonviolence and regarded the Bible as higher than human traditions.

Referring to the differences between the two faiths, Bishop Irineos said, "You Mennonites don't make much of Mary the mother of Jesus, do you? You don't have pictures and icons of her. You don't pray to her. But my people do. I teach them to. For us Mary is very important. It has just occurred to me that if you send us your teachers they might say things against Mary that would offend my people."

Dyck agreed that there might be a problem, but there need not be. "You are right," he said, "we don't worship Mary or the saints. We don't believe tradition is as important as the Bible. But why talk about something we are *against*? Why not talk about something we both agree on and have in common?" Dyck pointed out that both Mennonites and the Orthodox love Jesus and the church. If they concentrated on these things they had in common, they could work together and that way help the Cretans.

"If we send you teachers and helpers to Crete," Dyck proposed, "they'll come with clear instructions not to speak against Mary, the saints, or tradition. They'll speak about Jesus Christ. He's the one we love and serve. So we have nothing to disagree about."

Dyck flew back to Frankfurt, Germany, and submitted the Crete project to MCC central office in Akron, Pennsylvania. They agreed to send young men and women to Crete to help the people there with vocational training. It took some time before suitable volunteers could be found. Eventually Richard Kaufman, an electrician from Ohio, declared his willingness to serve with MCC in Crete. But he could not go immediately. However, Klaus Froese, a metallurgist from north Germany, was prepared to leave for Crete at once.

When Dyck examined the files and recommendations in support

of the two young men and saw their enthusiasm, he was overjoyed. Richard would teach the young men of Crete everything he knew about electricity, including wiring a house and repairing appliances. Klaus would teach students welding and grille work; skills needed for repairing farm machinery, oxcarts, and wagons; and how to build railings for steps in houses.

Klaus seemed an almost perfect volunteer. He was young, had the needed skills, was healthy and strong, had already worked on his own and gained valuable experience, and was a church member in good standing. Moreover, Klaus was ready to leave for Crete immediately and begin his work there.

One day about a month after Klaus Froese had left for Crete, Dyck was reading letters and reports concerning the many activities of MCC throughout the world. Suddenly he thought about Klaus in Crete and went pale.

"Peter Dyck, what have you done!" he moaned again and again. "How could you be so stupid? How could you send Klaus Froese to Crete? Klaus is a *German*! How could you forget that the Cretans *hate* the Germans?"

Immediately Dyck made arrangements to fly to Crete to see how Klaus was doing. When Dyck met Bishop Irineos and asked about the young German volunteer, the clergyman beamed and had nothing but good to say about Klaus. According to the bishop, Klaus was learning the Greek language and had begun to instruct young men in the art of metallurgy. When Dyck saw Klaus he found that the young man was happy and eager to do well, not only in teaching his skills, but also in young people's work.

Klaus worked hard, was meticulous and thorough in whatever he did, and took great pride in his achievements. Students liked him and were happy to learn a trade from him. When Richard Kaufman joined Klaus in Crete, the two young men established a vocational training school in the town of Kastelli. MCC also sent Orpha Zimmerli, equipped with a knitting machine and other tools, to teach the girls and women home economics. The bishop and the people of Kastelli were most pleased to see this developing vocational school in their midst.

The apprentice system was a good way to teach young people their vocational skills. When the students graduated from the various programs, they got jobs and even began to teach other young Cretans what they had learned. The so-called Klaus and Richard Vocational School did so well that the government officially recognized the school, erected a new building for it, and contributed money toward its operation. Enrollments increased and more staff had to be added.

When Klaus' two years were up, the bishop, the people of Kastelli, and, of course, the students, would not let him return to Germany. Arrangements were made for Klaus to stay for another two-year term.

When the second term ended, the people of Kastelli arranged a great farewell celebration for the young man who had done so much for them. There were many speeches in his honor. Bishop Irineos said, "Klaus Froese came to us as a gift from God." The mayor of Kastelli said, "When Klaus came, none of us knew him. We paid very little attention to him. Today he leaves us as a dear friend. We will all miss him."

Then came the surprise, at least for Klaus. The mayor announced, "We have decided to make you an honorary citizen of our town, Kastelli—for the rest of your life!" The people cheered, the band struck up the music, the students beamed with pride, and the mother of one of them wept for joy.

Back in Germany, Klaus became a social worker, taking care of more than 280,000 Greek migrant workers. He married Gudrun Wiebe, another German MCC worker in Greece. The couple have two daughters. When they go on vacation, they of course go to Crete where Klaus occupies a prominent place in the hearts of many Cretans.

As Peter Dyck writes, "Klaus Froese had done what more than 15,000 armed soldiers could not do. He had captured the hearts of the people of Crete. They had accepted him as one of their own. . . . The love and humble service of one young man had melted all their hatred and defenses. And he was a German."

41

The Battle of the Eyes

*T*welve o'clock.

"Gerhard Henrychovich, you're to appear in the administration office."

I walk to the administration office of the laboratory for state supervision of norms and measurement technology where I've been working for the last fifteen years. I'm told that, as one liable to serve in the military, I am to appear at 1:00 p.m. at the Second Division of the military commissariat. I am to bring my passport and temporary military release papers.

KGB! The thought flashes through my mind. The Committee for State Security. In the past this committee was called Political State Administration, or GPU for short. My father got to know this institution well during six years of imprisonment. Among ordinary citizens the three letters stood for "Gospodi, pomogi ubeshatj" (God, help me to get away), or, in reverse order, "Ubeshal, proslavlay Gospoda" (If you get away, praise God).

What do they want from me? There are, of course, many reasons for them wanting to see me. I'm German. I believe in God. My father is an elder in the Mennonite Brethren congregation. And I'm a choir leader and work with young people. Or have they perhaps discovered our Bible school?

These thoughts don't keep me from running home as fast as I can. I have to get the documents, and I'll have a chance to tell my

family where I'm going. But I can't be late, for it might count against
me. At home I tell my wife and mother to pray for me, grab the necessary documents, and rush to the bus which is to take me to my
hated destination.

"Good day! I've been ordered to appear before the Second Division."

"Your name?"

"Woelk."

"I know nothing about it."

"Then I can go?"

The receptionist looks more intently at me.

"Just a minute, I'll go and check. What was your name?"

"Woelk."

The lady disappears behind one of the doors and comes back immediately.

"They're expecting you."

I'm more calm. My heart no longer beats as fast as I enter one of the doors behind the receptionist.

"Good day!"

A man in his mid-fifties, in civilian clothes, rises behind his desk and extends his hand to me.

"Commandant Afanasyev. Good day! I've been waiting for you."

I look at him and decide he must know that I know who he is.

"There must be a mistake; I've been asked to appear before the Second Division—and you're not of that division."

"You're right. Nevertheless, it's I who have invited you. Please take a seat."

He leaves the door slightly ajar.

"Your papers, please!"

I hand him the dark-green passport and the red military document. I'm now in his hands—no, I'm in God's hands!

"Your name!"

"Woelk."

"First name!"

"Gerhard."

"Patronymic!"

"Henrychovich."

"Date of birth, place of birth!"

Usual questions. He does not look up as yet. He could get all the answers to his questions from the papers before him. He writes on a white sheet of paper. He takes another and continues writing. He pushes my documents to the corner of the desk. He no longer needs them. Only when I get them back will I be able to leave.

"Well, Gerhard Henrychovich, you're working at the state laboratory?"

"Yes, at the laboratory for state supervision." To be precise will not hurt!

"And you like your work?"

From now on he looks me straight in the eyes. I return his piercing look, keeping my eyes riveted to his. I must not yield and look away, not for a moment. That's what my father told me. He knows. Part of the struggle is fought with the eyes. Whoever lowers or even bats his eyes has lost half the battle.

"Thanks, I enjoy my work."

"And your salary? Isn't it a bit low?"

"It corresponds to my training."

"But you're an engineer, aren't you?"

"Yes."

"You have a family to support. A wife and four children. Couldn't you use a bit more?"

"My salary suffices."

I must not express dissatisfaction. Whatever you get from the state is okay. And I must answer simply, clearly, decisively. Most important, my answers must not help create a prolonged discussion. O God, grant me the necessary wisdom!

"And if we were to offer you twice as much?"

"My income suffices!"

"I mean in addition to what you're making now!"

"Thanks, we lack nothing."

He can't get anywhere and must change his tactic.

"Your profession takes you to many places, doesn't it? To factories, scientific institutions?"

"Yes, according to plans and schedules."

"And you no doubt see that here and there things are not in the best order or condition? That there are people who're not satisfied with the way things are? With your intelligence there's, of course, nothing that escapes you!"

Flattery. He smiles, I smile back. I feel the extreme tension, but he must not notice. We're just engaged in a friendly conversation. And whatever you do, keep looking him straight in the eyes.

"I'm not expected to do that."

"What do you mean?"

I must be more careful! My answers must not give rise to new questions.

"Intelligence work."

I can't say "spying"! That would be an insult to him.

"You're aiming too high, Comrade! It's information service. That's all it is."

"Nevertheless."

"What then are your duties?"

What does he expect me to say? The struggle of the eyes continues. Mutual smiles. The best of friends speak with one another.

"I'm a father of four children."

The mistake has been corrected. There are no new questions.

"What did you say your name was?"

"Woelk."

"And your first name?"

This is a well-known method. It will be repeated several times. It's a test of nerves.

"You're liable to serve in the military, aren't you?"

I cast a quick glance at the document on the desk. My eyes can rest a bit, but not for long. He has understood me, but still, I must give him an answer. But always as few words as possible.

"Yes."

"You then, of course, know that you're obligated to do all you can to serve state security."

"Do all service men have a side job with you?"

There will be no answer to this question of mine. I can now leave some of his questions unanswered as well.

"You of course know, Comrade, that no one must know what we're discussing here! Sign here, please, that you'll keep these things to yourself."

Under no circumstances! This way some have signed their death warrant. Or the death warrant of someone else. Our fathers and older brothers have told us about it. . . . Refuse to sign? Of course! But on what grounds? Well, officially this is not an interrogation, just a friendly conversation. It must remain that! Of course, there must be no challenge, no defiance. The semblance of equality between the discussion partners must remain intact.

"That I can't do, Comrade Commandant."

"But you're obligated!"

"My wife must not know either?"

It's always easier to ask questions.

"Naturally!"

"No, it's not natural. I don't want any mistrust to arise in my family. That happens easily when family members aren't open and honest with one another."

He tries to hide his anger. There's also a touch of curiosity in his
face.

"Do you really tell your wife everything?"

"Naturally!"

"Is it really a matter of course?"

"In a healthy marriage—yes!"

Seemingly a harmless dialogue between two friends. We smile
and apparently talk about unimportant things. But our eyes are
locked. Who will give in first? Who will win? O God, help me!

"And your wife?"

"What do you mean now?"

"Will she keep things to herself?"

"Well, she's not obliged not to talk."

"Nevertheless!"

I will not tell him that my wife can keep secrets to herself.

"She might talk to other people"

"What then shall we do?"

"Best of all, you tell nothing that my wife or anyone else shouldn't
know."

There's again hidden anger in his face. But he doesn't want to be
the first to lose composure.

"Your name!"

"Woelk."

"First name!"

Again these pointless questions.

"Tell me something about your father."

"What do you wish to know?"

"He's retired, isn't he?"

"Yes."

"What does he do with his time now?"

"Why are you interested?'

His eyes seem to say, *Will you answer me?* The corners of his
mouth are tired from smiling. The battle of the eyes continues. The
telephone rings. Only the caller speaks, whom I don't hear.

"Comrade Woelk, I've just been told that our room is needed. We'll have to continue our conversation in another room."

He rises. Will I get back my papers now? No, he takes them with him. He motions me to follow him downstairs. The doors here are much heavier than upstairs. For a moment my eyes can rest. He locks the door and puts the key into his pocket.

"So that we're not disturbed!"

He smiles, a bit awkwardly, I think. The room is semidark. . . . Keep open my eyes, the battle is not over yet. Again we smile at each other.

"Your name please!"

I must have a pleasant-sounding name! Why else repeat it so often!

"Are you prepared to assist us in our work?"

"My laboratory work and my family leave me little time for anything else."

"What we have talked here we'll keep to ourselves?"

"My wife will know about it."

"What work is your father doing?"

"He's on pension."

"Do you know that many Germans wish to emigrate to Germany?"

Oh! A new subject! I'll have to be careful!

"Yes."

"How do you feel about that?"

"Each person's business."

"Do you know anyone who wishes to leave?"

"You know them as well."

I hear the ticking of my wristwatch. The commandant repeats his questions. I must remain vigilant and careful—the shorter the answers, the better, in case I have to repeat them. Occasionally a new subject comes up, but nothing of importance.

The main issues have become clear to me. He expects me to accuse my brothers in the faith. That is why he tries to intimidate me. My family ought not to know about all of this. I'm to become a spy against my father and a traitor to my people. And for all this I would be paid well. It's getting late.

"Gerhard Henrychovich, our conversation has become somewhat long."

I agree. I have felt so for some time!

"But I suggest that we don't dot the 'i' as yet! We can, of course, continue some other time."

Oh, he knows German usage! The Russian 'i' has no dot!

"Comrade Commandant, I would suggest we dot the 'i' now!"

Our eyes are fighting the last battle. The extreme tension of nerves is covered up with friendliness and smiles.

"I'm sorry, no! You may go now!"

He hands me my documents. I turn to the door. In instances of this nature you don't say, "See you again!" I'm outside, I'm free. The calm I possessed inside leaves me now. I feel an extreme fatigue. It doesn't matter now. I'm happy it turned out well for me. I'm convinced God gave me the victory.

42

Keep It

*T*he Palatinate (Pfalz) on the west side of the Rhine River is one of the most beautiful regions in Germany. Whenever I travel there, I enjoy visiting the old and well-kept villages with their narrow streets and restaurants.

One day in June, I sat with friends around a table in a restaurant. Invariably my German friends talk about how the wine there is produced, what the descriptions on the labels mean, and about the breathtaking beauty of the Palatinate in general.

One friend said, "Would you like to know how the Palatinate got its name?"

As a student of history I was, of course, interested. I sat back to listen to his story.

"When our Lord was tempted by the devil in the desert," the friend began, "he was led to these regions along the Rhine River and shown the great beauty of the area. The devil then said to the Lord, 'If you will fall down and worship me, I will give you this region as your very own.'

"This was most tempting to the Lord, but being God himself who cannot sin, Jesus said to the devil, 'Dann p'halts!' [Then keep it!]. Ever since then," my friend laughingly concluded, "this state has been called Die Pfalz."

We all laughed. Then I said to my friends, "Your story underlines the fact that the Palatinate is so beautiful that even our Lord found it

so and was tempted by it. But I submit there could be another interpretation to your story. Do you want to hear it?"

When my friends agreed, I said, "The Palatinate is no doubt very
beautiful. But wouldn't you agree that, since the Lord did not take
possession of this state, it is at least conceivable that the devil is still
master over this region and the human activities in it?

"Think of the people here who find many occasions to celebrate
the new and old wine throughout the year. There are times the god
Bacchus is more in evidence than our Lord. It may be true that
there is 'truth in wine' (*in vino veritas*), but the truth of it is not always a godly one."

My friends laughed and said, "You're no doubt right, but we pre-
fer to emphasize the more positive part of the story about the origin
of the Palatinate."

"If I may," I said, "I would like to tell you something about my
people, who some centuries ago fled to these regions to escape
persecution in Switzerland."

My friends became more serious and prepared to listen. They
urged me to tell them the connection between the Palatinate and
the Mennonites.

"The Mennonites were received here better than elsewhere," I
began. "But here too they suffered hardships, discrimination, and
humiliation at the hands of state church people and society."

My Catholic and Protestant friends were all ears. The one who
had told the story about the name of their state moved his wine
glass aside and said, "Yes, I know, our people have not always dealt
justly with the Anabaptists. It's time we acknowledged this."

"As I said before," I continued, "your rulers in the seventeenth
century, the electors of the Palatinate, received many of the refugees from Switzerland and elsewhere kindly, even though they did
not agree with the religious faith of these people.

"But since these persecuted men and women were honest and
hard workers, the electors could use them to build up their towns,
villages, and the economy after the devastating wars. Many of the
villages, farmlands, and vineyards around here were built and developed by these grateful people. And the descendants of these
people still live here."

My friends named several "Mennonite" villages in the

region—Monsheim, Enkenbach, Deutschhof, Weierhof, and others.

"Beginning in 1717, under Elector Karl Philip," I resumed, "a determined effort was made to stop the spread of the Mennonite population throughout the Palatinate. No additional Mennonites were allowed in the region, the protection money the Mennonites had to pay for religious toleration was doubled, and the marriages of young people was made difficult. To get a marriage license, the parents of young people often had to approach the officials 'with their hands in their pockets,'—bribing them.

"Once the young couple was married and wished to start a farm, it was difficult to buy land because the government tried to limit the expansion of Mennonites as much as possible. For this purpose an ancient law, *ius retractus*, was revived and applied to the Mennonites. According to this law, land which had once been in Catholic, Lutheran, or Reformed hands, then was purchased by a Mennonite, could at any time be reclaimed by the original owner on payment of the original purchase price. Mennonites who had developed formerly worthless land into high productivity often lost their farms when an envious neighbor from one of the three tolerated religions decided to reclaim it."

"How unfair! Did you know this?" one of my friends exclaimed as he turned to the others.

"There was more to the persecution of Mennonites in this region," I continued. "Mennonites here were allowed to believe what they wished as long as they did not propagate their beliefs and practices among their neighbors. For example, as late as 1780, two young girls of Amish-Mennonite parentage were taken as orphans into a Catholic institution, baptized, then trained and educated as Catholics. When they became adults, they returned voluntarily to the church of their parents.

"The case was submitted for legal opinion to the Catholic section of the senate of the University of Heidelberg. The senate declared that the two young women were worthy of death for having left the Catholic church and joining the Mennonite. The elector, however, ruled that the two be imprisoned for a year and on their release be exiled. Hans Nafziger of Essingen, who had re-baptized the two young women, was ordered to pay a fine of five hundred florin and banished from the land."

"Can you imagine the stupid men at Heidelberg!" one friend burst out. "At least Heidelberg is no longer part of the Palatinate!" My friends chuckled.

"I shall tell you just one more story about the Mennonites in the Palatinate," I said. "Not only the living Mennonites were mistreated in these regions; the dead too were insulted and humiliated beyond measure. Since the Mennonites did not belong to the official religions, they were denied burial rights in the public cemeteries.

"A Mennonite of Kaiserslautern, for example, had died and was buried in the common burial ground of that city without the knowledge of the local priest, who was away on business. When the priest returned and heard that a Mennonite had been illegally interred in the cemetery, he called the local police. Together they dug up the body and buried it just outside the cemetery walls. As one chronicler suggests, this was done to show the Mennonites what the churches and the public thought of them."

My friends shook their heads. The earlier merry mood had vanished. At last one said, "I'm glad we're living today in more tolerant times. Here we are Catholics, Lutherans, Reformed, Mennonites, and even unbelievers—and we're all friends!"

We all laughed again, raised our glasses to our friendship, and resumed our conversation in a lighter vein.

One of my friends concluded: "We'll have to revise our story about the Lord, the devil, and the Palatinate. There is no doubt that the devil has been at work here for many centuries!"

43

A Courageous Mother

*A*t the time I was frightened and confused. I was young and did not fully understand what my mother experienced and suffered. Today as I remember my mother, I am angry about what men, Christian and non-Christian, did to her.

In 1937, during the height of the Soviet purges, my mother lost her husband, my father. I remember one night there was a knock on the window.

I heard Mother say to Father, "Now they have come to take you." Father got up, lit a lamp, dressed quickly, and opened the door. Mother also got up and dressed.

Two policemen entered the house. Opening drawers and closets, they searched for documents and other materials. After they had finished, they took Father by the arms and led him away. Mother stretched out her arms toward him and wept uncontrollably.

One policemen turned and said, "Don't cry, your husband will soon be back."

Defiance in her voice, my mother snapped, "Don't give me that! I know how he'll come back! He'll never return!"

And Father didn't come back. At first mother visited him in the nearby prison to which three months earlier my grandfather had been taken. Both Father and Grandfather were tortured until they agreed to sign the trumped-up charges against them. Then they were sent to one of the many labor camps which dotted the vast Siberian regions.

Many years later, in Canada, my mother received news from the Red Cross in Moscow that Father had perished sometime in the 1940s. While many other women had to live with uncertainty about their husband's fate, Mother at least knew that Father no longer suffered.

For my mother difficult times now began. She worked hard on the collective farm to keep her three children and mother-in-law fed and clothed. She taught us children how to pray and to believe in God and Christian values. During the war and the great trek west, she did all in her power to hold her family together and provide our daily necessities. No matter how scarce food was, we never went hungry.

Mother was still young during the war years. She loved life in spite of the tragedies that had overtaken her. She read books and attended occasional concerts. She even took me to a movie one day. The film was called *Elisabeth,* I remember, and dealt with love and marriage. During the movie my mother sobbed, trying to hide her tears from me. On the way home, we did not talk much, but I remembered how one evening my father played the violin and mother sang a Russian song. The song was about a young woman's longing for her distant lover who served his country as a soldier.

By the end of the war, our family—Mother and three of us children—had come as far as the Elbe River. Many other refugees also hoped to cross to the British zone so as to escape the Red Army. However, one day Cossacks on horseback appeared along the dikes, ordering the refugees away from the river. My mother worried about our being sent back to the Soviet Union, but thanks to her intelligence, courage, and daring, we eventually escaped to the West. A new life began for all of us.

After the war, congregational life in Germany was organized again. For the first time in my life, I attended a Mennonite church. The few men who had survived the 1930s and 1940s—some had served in the Soviet, German, or both armies—now took over leadership in the refugee congregations. As they had prior to the Mennonite collapse in Russia, they again preached, admonished, and taught the Christian way.

The women, who had come through difficult times, submitted and followed as they had before. One day my mother had to appear

before the congregation and repent for the "worldly" life she had lived during the war years. Mother submitted humbly and apologized for having "failed the Lord" repeatedly over the years. She was, of course, forgiven and restored to full fellowship in the congregation. Other women had to do the same. Even then, young as I was, I wondered why Mother and other women were treated this way.

In 1948 we emigrated to Canada. We joined a Mennonite congregation in western Canada. The sermons we heard, preached by respected male lay ministers, dealt with such externals as dress codes, length of hair, silk stockings, and other things pertaining to women, not men. I never heard my mother complain about the preachers' harping on women's behavior, and she certainly did not rebel against any church rules. She no doubt came to believe that the Mennonite way in Canada was the way of the Lord. And she taught us children to submit obediently to the church as well.

At the beginning in Canada, Mother still read books, some from the church library. But eventually prayer meetings and Bible studies replaced all other reading. To attend concerts or movies was, of course, out of the question at the time.

In the end my mother remarried, moved to the Canadian West Coast, and was integrated into Mennonite social and communal life. She changed her name and identity. As she aged, I recognized her less and less as the woman she had been. Suffering from loss of memory and haunted by fears, she tried to escape from the senior citizens home. They tied her down. A few years ago, death came quickly and mercifully.

I'm still angry. Not because my father and mother, like so many others, had to endure untold hardships. I try to understand those difficult times in the context of history and our people's existence within it. Nor am I all that angry because my mother lost her husband and I my father, while other men escaped that cruel fate and later began a new life in a new country. What I *am* angry about is what the leading men in Mennonite communities did to my mother and other women—all in the name of religious faith and submission to the Lord.

As I reflect on those years, I realize it was the women, not the men, who kept the faith and Mennonite values alive at great risk and danger to themselves. The mothers and grandmothers maintained family life when all organized congregational existence had come to an end. And when the men returned after the war, they not only resumed their former leadership in the congregations but also made the women feel guilty about how they had lived during times of hardship. And my mother and women like her did not rebel against the "brethren" and their ways! Should I be angry about this as well?

But may Mother rest in peace! In my memory I will try no longer to hear her apologize for the way she lived. I will remember her as a courageous young woman who talked back to the policemen, who toiled and suffered for her children, who read books and took me to a movie.

44

Should George and Anna Evangelize Europe?

*M*y friend George and his wife, Anna, have been missionaries in an area of Europe that is predominantly Roman Catholic. Having attended Mennonite institutions and served as a pastor couple in several congregations in Canada, George and Anna accepted an invitation from the Mennonite Brethren mission board to plant churches and serve as Bible teachers in Europe.

The mission work was slow and often discouraging. However, with time small fellowship groups were established and some became Mennonite Brethren congregations. Thus in countries where some five centuries ago the Anabaptists, forebears of the Mennonites, were cruelly persecuted by the Roman Catholic Church and society, there is now again, however small, an Anabaptist witness.

In numerous discussions and letters, George, Anna and I have debated the question of mission work among people and in countries which consider themselves Christian. I have my reservations about doing mission work among European people, especially with the aim of converting them to the Mennonite faith. George and Anna, however, are convinced that evangelism and missions among Roman Catholics is both necessary and in line with Christ's mandate to go into all the world to preach the gospel to all people.

On a recent visit to George and Anna, who live amidst beautiful surroundings in southern Europe, a dialogue between my friends and me developed.

"It seems to me," I began, "that the Mennonite Brethren conference should follow the General Conference (GC) of Mennonites in not designating Europe as their mission field. The GCs believe that European countries have a Christian witness. Hence it is not necessary to spend time, effort, and money doing work that others, especially their own people, should be and possibly are doing."

George was ready with an answer. "I don't agree with that policy for several reasons. First, the people here, although Catholic, are very superstitious, live in spiritual darkness, and have moral needs which must be met. I have met men and women who have not been helped by their church. These people come to us and we tell them about the Jesus who forgives sin, heals, and restores broken lives.

"Second, we missionaries are simply obedient to the great commission of our Lord to go into *all* the world. This includes European countries as much as non-Christian countries."

"Don't you think," I said, "that to steal sheep from another fold is questionable at best? This spiritual poaching smacks not only of intolerance but also arrogance. By trying to win Catholics over to your side, you're saying in effect that you have the whole truth whereas the Catholics don't. Surely today, in an age of greater tolerance and acceptance of others, such an attitude reveals a closed mind, even bigotry."

"I don't think we're stealing sheep, as you put it," Anna said, visibly annoyed. "We're merely inviting these people to listen to what we have to say. If they think we can help them, they may join our fellowship. It's entirely their decision."

"Frankly, Anna, the Catholic societies and governments are more tolerant than we are. They did not invite you to come to them, yet they allow you to propagandize your faith among them. How would we feel if Jesuits, for example, were to come to Winnipeg or the Fraser Valley to evangelize among our Mennonites there? I don't think we would receive them with open arms, would we?"

Anna and George shifted in their chairs and just looked at me, evidently not having thought about this reverse situation before.

"I must admit," I continued, "that I have real difficulties with the concept of evangelism and church planting among fellow Christians. Who am I to say that my understanding of the Christian faith is right and that of other groups is wrong? Does it really matter whether one believes according to a Mennonite confession of faith or another Protestant or Catholic creed? The important thing is, surely, that we all live according to the gospel of love, and in this all Christian creeds agree."

"Are you suggesting," George said, "that we should do away with all denominational differences and retain only those beliefs and practices which all Christian groups have in common? This kind of ecumenism will never happen. Nor should it, for it would reduce our Christian faith to the lowest common denominator and lead to a shallow faith and Christian life."

"No, I'm not suggesting that we do away with all denominational distinctives," I said. "On the contrary, what I'm saying is that we should accept and respect the various Christian denominations. Instead of evangelizing among them, we should learn from their traditions and insights. In this regard I'm impressed with the position the Russian Mennonites took around the turn of this century. They—"

"What can we really learn from the Russian Mennonites about missions?" George interrupted. "As far as I know, they were not much concerned about mission work in Russia. Had they not promised the Russian government they would not evangelize among the Russian Orthodox population?"

"It is true that the newcomers to Russia were not allowed to make converts among the Orthodox, but the Mennonites never promised, nor were they required to make a promise that they would not evangelize among Russian believers. But what I was going to say—the Russian Mennonites held some fairly mature views with regard to other Christian denominations, views from which we can learn."

"What do you mean?" Anna asked with obvious interest.

"According to P. M. Friesen's history," I said, "our forebears in Russia certainly believed in the Lord's mandate to proclaim the good news to all people. But they refrained—and this is important—from propagandizing their beliefs among other Christian groups. This at least was their official position. Unofficially, however, there were mission workers, especially among the MBs, who risked imprisonment and exile for preaching to and baptizing Russian-Orthodox people."

"I'm with those who had the courage to be faithful to the Lord of harvest and had a heart for the lost Russians," Anna said with satisfaction. "But tell me, how did the Russian Mennonites justify their official position, as you put it? Surely, they had no biblical basis for their lack of mission spirit!"

"Perhaps not chapter and verse," I said, "but it seems to me that they acted in the spirit of Christ's love and tolerance. Friesen—"

"This I would like to see explained," George interrupted again. He sat back and grinned.

"Just hear me out; Friesen explains the position of the Russian Mennonites like this. The Mennonites will evangelize and seek to win converts among non-Christian people and in countries where there is no Christian witness. And we know that the Russian Mennonites supported mission work in India, for example, and even sent missionaries to that subcontinent. But they refrained from mission work among fellow believers because they respected the Christian faith, no matter what form it took.

"As Friesen puts it, the full Christian truth is not found in the individual parts but in the combination of the many Christian creeds and expressions of faith. Each part, or each denomination, if you will, thus makes a valuable contribution to the truth of the gospel. As Mennonites, for example, we too have valuable insights to add to the Christian confession, insights not as common among other Christian groups."

"What insights, for example?" George wanted to know.

"The emphasis on peace in all areas of life," I said, "on brotherhood and community, and on following Jesus in the practical affairs of life. As a historic peace church, our witness among fellow Christians is a valuable contribution to what Christian faith is all about."

"If this is so," Anna said, "shouldn't we seek to win to our particular faith and life other so-called Christians who do not share these truths?"

"If other believers want to join our congregations, we, of course, will not reject them but take them in, as Friesen observes. But we should not, I believe, go out to convert them to our particular Christian faith and plant our churches in the midst of other Christian communities. To dialogue and cooperate with them is another matter. There is much we can teach them and much we can learn from them, don't you think?"

George shifted uneasily in his chair, looked at Anna and cast a glance in the direction of the kitchen where the evening meal was cooking. Turning to me, he said, "Much of what you say makes good sense, but you still have not explained what it means to take Christ's great commission seriously today."

"I don't have all the answers," I said, "but it seems to me that the 'go ye into all the world' must not be interpreted too narrowly. First, Jesus spoke those words at a time when the Christian faith had not spread as yet. The disciples were told to make the message of Christ's love and forgiveness known throughout the world, which they did.

"Second, to teach people the things the disciples had learned of Jesus included practical expressions of faith, such as helping the poor and oppressed people. Remember what Jesus says in Matthew 25? He doesn't talk there about what we believe but about what his followers have done for others. He tells us there that what we have done for the hungry, sick, and destitute, we have done for Jesus."

"Don't you think you're coming dangerously close to the old social gospel emphasis and mere humanism as a substitute for faith?" George asked.

"I hope not, George," I said, "but I do believe that the good news of the gospel must include the human, material, and social well-being of people. This is why I believe our foreign mission work in places like India has helped the people there both spiritually and socially."

"So you do believe in propagandizing our Christian faith among the heathen and unchurched!" Anna exclaimed triumphantly.

"Of course," I said, "but hear me out, please. In India our missionaries worked among people, the outcasts, whom their upper classes or castes had abandoned and relegated to a most wretched existence. The gospel not only gave them faith but also human dignity and a life worth living for."

"The same can be said about the Catholic converts in Europe," Anna said. "Where there was little or no hope for these Catholics, there is now faith, a sense of belonging, and purpose for living."

"I don't doubt it," I said, "but what I am saying is that the Christians in these European countries have the Christian message and it is their—not our—responsibility to proclaim and apply the gospel to their people and needs."

"Should we then abandon Europe altogether, just because the countries there are nominally Christian?" Anna asked.

"There is work for Mennonites in Europe as well. Together with European Mennonites we can and should work among our people who have left the Soviet Union in the last decades and resettled in Germany. They—"

"I agree," George interrupted again, "but it is very difficult to change these people's ways. They are most conservative, set in their religious habits, even legalistic about outward things such as length of hair, head covering for the women, and other things."

"I see what you mean, but isn't that all the more reason for helping them if they want our help? I know they want our assistance and cooperation so long as we don't come to them as people who know it all. Besides, we can learn much from the simple and steadfast faith of our brothers and sisters from the Soviet Union."

Visibly troubled, George said, "We certainly could do more for our Russian Mennonites and work more closely together with them. I remain uneasy, however, about your idea not to evangelize among European Catholics and Protestants."

"Well, here we come back to the beginning of our conversation," I said. "My point simply is that we need to respect the beliefs and ways of other Christians. We're not responsible for the problems of the whole world. However, we are responsible for our 'neighbors,'—those closest to us at home and abroad, and also for those who really need to be helped."

George stood and said, "I'm sure we haven't solved the problem of missions. We'll have to continue talking in the hope of finding a better way. Perhaps after we've eaten?"

George took Anna's hand and motioned to the dining room.

"I agree," I said as I followed my friends. Smiling I added, "As Brecht says, 'Nach dem Essen geht alles besser' (All things go better after one has eaten)."

George laughed and said, "Harry, I always knew you were a humanist—quoting that Marxist writer!"

We all laughed and sat down to eat.

45

A Conversation
on the Train

*E*arly in October, 1990, just after German unification, I traveled by train between Weimar and Mannheim. I had visited places associated with Johann Wolfgang Goethe, the great German poet of classical beauty and harmony. In the train compartment were three other travelers.

Sitting beside me was a young man of about thirty years. He was talkative and expressive, especially when it came to the subject of German unification and what that might mean for Germany's future and the world.

Across from me sat an elderly couple, the man about seventy-five and his wife some fifteen years younger. Bald, flat-chested, with a protruding belly, the man was hard of hearing and opinionated. His wife seemed good-natured, more cautious in expressing her views and somewhat motherly in her bearing. The couple had visited relatives in Leipzig and were now on their way home to Frankfurt.

When I joined the trio in Weimar, they were engaged in animated conversation about the dilapidated conditions in the former German Democratic Republic and how much money and effort it would take to raise East German conditions to West German levels.

"And who will pay for all this?" the old man asked.

"We the taxpayers, of course," the woman said nodding to the young man beside me.

The young man agreed but added, "We'll manage things. Just

give us time. Besides, the East Germans will do their part as well."

Not wishing to join in a conversation whose subject I heard discussed almost every day, I looked out the window and thought about the history of the area through which I was traveling. Weimar, Jena, Erfurt, Eisenach—places filled with historical, cultural, and literary meaning and significance. Luther, Goethe, the Weimar Republic, and more recent history, particularly the Third Reich, came to mind.

I was jolted out of my reverie when the conversation took a sudden and surprising turn. The old man suddenly said loudly and clearly, "Much of Germany's past troubles stem from the influence the Jews had in our history."

The woman nudged her husband with her elbow in an apparent attempt to halt his diatribe.

The man, however, became quite animated and continued, "I know what I'm talking about. In Frankfurt, for example, the Jews are again in influential positions. This does not bode well for Germany. Don't misunderstand me, I was not a Nazi during Hitler's time, not even a member of the party. But I can understand our peoples' fear of the Jews."

The young man mumbled something awkwardly and soon turned toward the window, apparently trying to sleep. The wife of the man was visibly embarrassed and tried to change the subject but without success.

Speaking ever louder, the man cited examples of Jews he had known and how they were not to be trusted. "They're not like other people. It's a different race. They have caused trouble wherever they were. Why are they hated by all others?" he asked rhetorically. Then turning to me, he asked what I thought about what he was saying. "You haven't said anything yet. Don't you think I'm right?"

Thus challenged I could not help but respond. I knew the man's attitude was not uncommon among German people. Most, however, did not express their anti-Semitism as crassly as this man.

In a low, calm voice, I said, "Since I'm not a German citizen but a Canadian, I would rather not become involved in talk about a subject painful to many people and which affects the Jews even today. But if you like, I'll tell you a bit about myself and some of my experiences during the last World War."

The old man, taken by surprise, said I should speak. His wife and the young man beside me encouraged me as well and prepared to listen.

I told them I belonged to a minority group called Mennonites. My forebears had suffered persecution in Europe, beginning in the sixteenth century and continuing well into modern times. Like the Jews, the Mennonites wandered from place to place in search of a homeland, or at least a place where they might be tolerated.

"I understand the Jews at least in part," I said. "The Jews have suffered much throughout their history, often at the hands of those who call themselves Christian."

Trying to defend his position, the old man said, "I don't know the Mennonites, but I know Jews and what they have done. Didn't the Jews hate Christ and in the end kill him? And have they not opposed our Christian faith and the church throughout history? Already our Luther warned us 'against the Jews and their lies.' " (He was referring to a work Luther had written in 1543.)

"I am much younger than you," I said, "but I remember the last world war well and what happened at the time. When the German armies invaded the Soviet Union in 1941, our people who lived in the Ukraine welcomed them as liberators from Communism. The Communists had destroyed our way of life, including our religious institutions, and in the 1930s our women lost their husbands through arrests and exiles. I too lost my father that way.

"The Germans, we believed, were God-fearing people who would restore our way of life and extend justice to all people. Even on their belts German soldiers carried the beautiful words 'God with us.' But we found that German godliness was different from what we thought about God and humanity."

The old man shifted restlessly in his seat. "I, of course, don't approve of what the Germans under Hitler did to many Jews, although I doubt it was six million that the Nazis exterminated," the man said.

Ignoring the comment I continued, "I must tell you about my grandmother, a woman who taught me to believe in God even though in Soviet schools we were taught that there was no God. As I said, with the coming of the Germans, we believed that faith in God and human values would be respected. But things turned out otherwise. The German army rounded up Jewish men and women, even children, and took them away from their homes. The victims' property was confiscated and much of it was taken by other people. One day my school friend, a Jew, disappeared as well."

The young man beside me said, "We can imagine what happened to them."

"Yes," I said, "they were taken several kilometers from our village. There they were shot into mass graves and buried. That's at least what we heard from people who had no reason to spread false reports. When we heard this, we were shocked. 'What did these people do to deserve such cruel fate?' we asked."

"Well," the old man interrupted me, "they must have been guilty of some crime, just like the Communists who arrested and exiled your father and other Germans."

"Please let the gentleman continue," the woman exclaimed impatiently to her husband. Turning to me, the woman said, "I think there is more about your grandmother in the story, isn't there?"

"Yes, my grandmother expressed an attitude at that time for which I'll always be grateful. It was in the afternoon. My grandmother was lying in her bed with another of her frequent headaches.

"She called me to her bedside and said, 'Harry, what the Germans are doing to the poor Jewish people is terrible. There is no doubt that this will some day come back to haunt them.'

"As you see, my grandmother, as much as she appreciated the Germans for having liberated us from Soviet Communism, was not blind to their unjust and inhuman treatment of other people. Today we all know that my grandmother was right."

After a pause I went on. "I might add that when we came to Germany toward the end of the war and told our German neighbors what the German army was doing in the east, they would not believe us. 'Impossible,' they said, 'our führer would never do such things.'"

The old man took his eyes off me and looked out the window. The other two were silent and looked out the window as well. Just then the Wartburg castle near Eisenach came into view. High above the Thuringian forest, the outlines of this imposing, history-laden structure were barely visible in the fading light outside.

Turning to the old man, I said, "You mentioned the German reformer Luther before. True, he wrote against the 'obstinate' Jews who refused to become Christians and suggested that they be exiled and their synagogues closed down. Luther expressed an attitude that was quite prevalent at the time. He no doubt contributed to the anti-Semitism among his people and others who followed his theology. Luther, by the way, also had some bad things to say about the rebellious peasants and the Anabaptists, our spiritual forebears. He even advocated that they be killed."

"But weren't those different times?" the woman asked. "Weren't people then less tolerant toward persons and groups who opposed the established order?"

"Yes, no doubt," I said, "but don't you think that a man of God like Luther should have patterned his thought and life more closely after Christ whom he represented and preached? And do you really think things today have changed all that much? After all these centuries since the Reformation, intolerance and hatred of other races and groups hasn't decreased."

Looking at the old man, I concluded, "Even after the Holocaust, there are still persons who call themselves Christians and at the same time hate other races, including the Jews."

It had become completely dark outside. With the light in the compartment, the faces of the occupants were clearly reflected in the window. In silence each one of us followed his own train of thought. The clatter of the train wheels continued.

At last the young man said, "Yes, that's how things were and are."

The woman sighed deeply and said, "Yes, we're all guilty and lack the Christian love we so loudly profess. Perhaps there's more hope with the young. We're too old to learn and to change." She looked at her husband.

All he said was, "Perhaps you're right."

At Hanau the young man got off. "Thanks for the story," he said and shook my hand.

As the train pulled into Frankfurt a few minutes later, the woman commented, "It's nice to be home. I'll sleep so well tonight." She pressed my hand and smiled.

As they left the compartment, the old man said "Aufwiedersehn!" without looking at me.

I transferred to another train which took me to Mannheim.

Sources

Chapter 1: The Radical Disturber
I reconstructed this story primarily from *Quellen zur Geschichte der Täufer in der Schweiz*, vol. 1, edited by Leonhard von Muralt (Zürich: S. Hirzel Verlag, 1952), pp. 37-39; George H. Williams, *The Radical Reformation* (Philadelphia: The Westminster Press, 1975), pp. 120-127; and John Allen Moore, *Anabaptist Portraits* (Scottdale, Pa.: Herald Press, 1984), pp. 17-93.

Chapter 2: The Doubting Priest
The Complete Writings of Menno Simons c. 1496-1561, trans. from the Dutch by Leonard Verduin and edited by John C. Wenger, with a biography by Harold S. Bender (Herald Press, 1956).

Chapter 3: The Little Swan of Emden
The Mennonite Encyclopedia, vol. 3, 305; vol. 4, 665-666 (Herald Press, 1957, 1959); *The Complete Writings of Menno Simons*, pp. 1050-1063.

Chapter 4: The Tragedy of a Woman
Die Wiedertäufer zu Münster Berichte, Aussagen und Aktenstücke von Augenzeugen und Zeitgenossen (Jena: Eugen Diederichs, 1923), pp. 232-233.

Chapter 5: No Man Ever Touched Me
Thieleman J. van Braght, *Martyrs Mirror* (Herald Press, 1950), pp. 481-482; A. Brons. *Ursprung, Entwickelung und Schicksale der altevangelischen Taufgesinnten oder Mennoniten in kurzen Zügen übersichtlich dargestellt* (Emden: Th. Halm Wwe., 1912), pp. 89-92.

Chapter 6: No Permanent City
M.P. "Die Vertriebenen. Eine Gischichte aus alten Zeiten," *Christlicher Gemeindekalender*, 1915, pp. 47-61.

Chapter 7: Exiles

P. M. Friesen, *Die Alt-Evangelische Mennonitische Brüderschaft in Russland (1789-1910), Teil II, Die Mennoniten in Nord-Amerika* (Halbstadt, Taurien: Verlagsgesellschaft 'Raduga,' 1911), pp. 118-122. Friesen took his account from Ernst Müller, "Langnaurer Täufer vor 200 Jahren," in *Mennonitische Blätter*, 1893, No. 19.

Chapter 8: An Ugly Affair

The Chronicle of the Hutterian Brethren, vol. 1. Trans. and ed. the Hutterian Brethren (Rifton, N.Y.: Plough Publishing House, 1987), pp. 723-731; *Das Klein-Geschichtsbuch der Hutterischen Brüder*. Hrsg. A.J.F. Zieglschmid (Philadelphia: The Carl Schurz Memorial Foundations, Inc., 1947), pp. 168-172; Peter Brock, *Freedom from Violence: Sectarian Nonresistance from the Middle Ages to the Great War* (Toronto: Univ. of Toronto Press, 1991). pp. 58-62; Robert Friedmann, "An Anabaptist Ordinance of 1633 on Nonresistance," *The Mennonite Quarterly Review* (April, 1951), pp. 116-127.

Chapter 9: Dreamer and Visionary

Leland Harder, "Pioneer of Christian Civilization in America," *Mennonite Life*, vol. 4 (Jan. 1949), No. 1, pp. 41-45, 48; Irvin B. Horst, "Pieter Cornelisz Plockhoy: An Apostle of the Collegiants," *The Mennonite Quarterly Review*.(July, 1949), pp. 161-185.

Chapter 10: A Teacher with a Heart

The Mennonite Encyclopedia, vol. 2, (1956) pp. 76-77; Gerald C. Studer, *Christopher Dock: Colonial Schoolmaster* (Herald Press, 1967).

Chapter 11: A Sunday in Pennsylvania

Karl Goetz in Horst Penner, *Weltweite Brüderschaft. Ein Mennonitisches Geschichtsbuch*, 2. Auflage (Karlsruhe: Verlag Heinrich Schneider, 1960), pp. 172-173.

Chapter 12: The Story of Christian Funk

Richard K. MacMaster with Samuel L. Horst and Robert F. Ulle, *Conscience in Crisis. Mennonites and Other Peace Churches in America, 1739-1789*. Interpretation and Documents (Herald Press, 1979); John L. Ruth, *Maintaining the Right Fellowship: A Narrative Account of Life in the Oldest Mennonite Community in North America* (Herald Press, 1984); C. Henry Smith, *The Mennonites: A Brief History of Their Origin and Later Development in Both Europe and America* (Berne, Ind.: Mennonite Book Concern, 1920); *The Mennonite Encyclopedia*, vol. 2, pp. 421-422; *Mennonitisches Lexikon*, vol. 2, pp. 19-21.

Chapter 13: The Story of a Book

The Mennonite Encyclopedia, vol. 3, (1957) pp. 423-424, 527-528; John L. Ruth, *Maintaining the Right Fellowship*; Gerald C. Studer, "A History of the *Martyrs Mirror*," *Mennonite Quarterly Review XXII* (July 1948), No. 3, pp. 163-179.

Chapter 14: Gold Coins for the Journey

Orland Gingerich, *The Amish of Canada* (Herald Press, 1972); John A. Hostetler, *Amish Society* (Baltimore, Md.: The John Hopkins University Press, 1980).

Chapter 15: Kidnapped

Jacob Krehbiel, "Der Bubendieb," *Jugendblätter*, 1865-1869; Emma K. Bachmann, "Der Bubendieb. A Kidnapping in the Olden Days," *Mennonite Life*, vol. 12 (July 1957), 3:131-132. In Bachmann's summary of the story, there are a number of inaccurate deviations from the original.

Chapter 16: How to Butter Up a King

C. Henry Smith, *The Story of the Mennonites*. Fifth edition, revised, and enlarged by Cornelius Krahn (Newton, Kan.: Faith and Life Press, 1981), pp. 177-179; J. Ellenberger, hrsg. *Bilder aus dem Pilgerleben*. Gesammelt in der Mennoniten-Gemeinde (Stuttgart: Selbstverlag des Verfassers, 1878-1883).

Chapter 17: Spies

J. Ellenberger, "Gefangennahme und Gefangenschaft der Gebrüder Böhr, auf dem Gaisberg bei Weissenburg, in Jahre 1870," in *Bilder aus dem Pilgerleben*, vol. 2 (Selbstverlag des Verfassers, 1880), pp. 109-120; Agathe Schotter, "Bärbel. Barbara Dick-Böhr 1859-1912. Die Geschichte eines Geisberger Mädchen, dass nach Russland heiratete." Typewritten manuscript with footnotes by Hans Hege, Reichshoffen, n.p, n.d.; Harry Loewen, trans. and ed., "Recollections of the Franco-German War, 1870-1871, by Barbara (Boehr) Dick," *Journal of Mennonite Studies*, vol. 7, 1989, pp. 33-50.

Chapter 18: Wine-Tasting

J. Ellenberger, hrsg., *Bilder aus den Pilgerleben*. Gesammelt in der Mennoniten-Gemeinde (Stuttgart: Selbstverlag des Verfassers, 1878-1883). I am grateful to Gary Waltner for making a copy of the story available to me.

Chapter 19: A Volunteer to Fight Napoleon

Reiswitz and Wadzeck, *Beiträge zur Kenntnis der Mennoniten-Gemeinden in Europa und Amerika, statistischen, historischen und religiösen Inhalts* (Berlin 1821), pp. 233-315; P. M. Friesen, *The Mennonite Brotherhood in Russia, 1789-1910* (revised edition, Hillsboro, Kan.: Kindred Press, 1980), p. 58.

Chapter 20: For Conscience' Sake

Adapted from a typewritten manuscript of a report by Elder Peter Bartel prepared in 1868. I am grateful to Pastor Peter J. Foth of the Mennonite Church in Hamburg and Altona who made the document available to me.

Chapter 21: Dispute About Wigs

Horst Quiring, "Der Danziger Perückenstreit," *Christlicher Gemeinde-Kalender*, 1936, pp. 98-102.

Chapter 22: A Politician

Ernst Crous, "Hermann von Beckerath," *Mennonitische Geschichtsblätter*, NeueFolge, Nr. 15, Jahrgang 20, 1963: 12-20; Christian Neff, "Beckerath, Hermann von," *Mennonitisches Lexikon* vol. 1, 150; *The Mennonite Encyclopedia*, vol. 1 (1955) 259; R. Schwemer and H. S. Bender, "Frankfurt Parliament," *The Mennonite Encyclopedia*, vol. 2 (1956) 376-377.

Chapter 23: Gift from a Woman's Hand

Anna Brons, *Upsprung, Entwickelung und Schicksale der altevangelischen Taufgesinnten oder Mennoniten in kurzen Zügen übersichtlich dargestellt von Frauenhand* (Norden, 1884); H. G. Mannhardt, "Endlich haben wir eine 'Geschichte der

Mennoniten,' " *Mennonitische Blätter* 32 (Jan. 1885), Nr. 1:4, Nr. 2, 11-12; Julia Hildebrant, "Antje Brons als Mennonitin," *Mennonitische Geschichtsblätter* 23, Neue Folge, Nr. 18, 1966: 41-58; H. van der Smissen, "Brons, Anna," *Mennonitisches Lexikon*, vol. 1:271-273. See also the article by the same author in *The Mennonite Encyclopedia*, vol. 1 (1955) 436-437.

Chapter 24: In the Face of Death
Gerhard G. Klassen, "Ereignisse aus dem 17. Jahrhundert" [sic], *Der Botschafter*, 9:17 (Feb. 28/March 13, 1914), p. 2.

Chapter 25: Visits from the Tsar
P. M. Friesen, *The Mennonite Brotherhood in Russia 1789-1910*, pp. 173-175, 193-194.

Chapter 26: The Ban
P. M. Friesen, *The Mennonite Brotherhood in Russia 1789-1910*, pp. 197-198.

Chapter 27: Sheer Madness
Franz Bartsch, *Unser Auszug nach Mittelasien* (Halbstadt, 1907); Fred Richard Belk, *The Great Trek of the Russian Mennonites to Central Asia 1880-1884* (Herald Press, 1976); C. Henry Smith, *The Story of the Mennonites* (Newton, Kan: Mennonite Publication Office, 1950); Walter Klaassen, "Apocalypticism," *The Mennonite Encyclopedia*, vol. 5, pp. 28-30.

Chapter 28: Thieves and Murderers
Fred Richard Belk, *The Great Trek of the Russian Mennonites to Central Asia, 1880-1884*, pp. 152-153, 163-167.

Chapter 29: Flight Across the River
Abram Friesen and Abram J. Loewen, *Die Flucht über den Amur*. Historische Schriftenreihe, Buch 2 (Rosthern, Sask. and Steinbach, Man.: Echo-Verlag, 1946).

Chapter 30: A Love Story
Peter J. Klassen, *Die Geschichte des Ohm Klaas* (Regina, Sask.: The Western Printers Ass'n. Ltd., n.d.). Klassen has no doubt fictionalized this story.

Chapter 31: The First Train Ride
"Die erste Eisenbahnfahrt. Ein heiteres Erlebnis." *Christlicher Gemeinde-Kalender* (43), 1934, pp. 91-97.

Chapter 32: The Canary
"Der Kanarienvogel," *Volksfreund* [*Friedensstimme*] II (XI) Jahrgang (7. März 1918), Nr. 8(26):4-6.

Chapter 33: Condemned to Die
P[eter] M[artin] F[riesen], "Ein mennonitischer Schächer. Drei Briefe," *Vorwärts-Kalender* für das Jahr unseres Herrn 1939:47-54; F. C. Thiessen, "P. M. Friesen," *Mennonitische Rundschau* 70 (19. März 1947), 12:2; 70(26. März 1946), 13:2; F. C. Thiessen, "My Recollections of P. M. Friesen," *Mennonite Life*, vol. 3 (October, 1948), 4:8-10, 45.

Chapter 34: The Church Took Her Children
Cornelius C. Peters, "Es war einmal ein Mensch . . . Einiges aus dem Leben von Cornelius C. Peters," *Mennonitische Rundschau*, May 9, 1973, p. 14; May 16, 1973, p. 14; Franz C. Peters, "Schw[ester] Anna Peters," obituary, *Mennonitische Rundschau*, Sept. 23, 1953; Franz Isaac, *Die Molotschnaer Mennoniten. Ein Beitrag zur Geschichte derselben* (Halbstadt, Taurien: H. J. Braun, 1908). Valuable document relating to the landless in Russia; Anne (Peters) Bargen, interviews, Sept. and Nov. 1990, Kelowna, British Columbia. I am grateful to Peter and Anne Bargen, who drew my attention to the story of their grandmother.

Chapter 35: Our Russian Maid
Translated and adapted from Helene Janzen, "Marija—unser russisches Mädchen," *Mennonite Mirror* 19 (Oct. 1989), 2:25-26. I am grateful to James Urry for suggesting this story to me.

Chapter 36: Whose Land?
Lawrence Klippenstein, "Mennonite Métis and Mennonite Immigrants: First Contacts," *The Mennonite Quarterly Review* XLVIII (Oct. 1974), 4:476-488; Leo Driedger, "Native Rebellion and Mennonite Invasion: An Examination of Two Canadian River Valleys," *The Mennonite Quarterly Review* XLVI (July 1972), 290-300; Henry J. Gerbrandt, *Adventure in Faith. The Background in Europe and the Development in Canada of the Bergthaler Mennonite Church of Manitoba* (Altona, Manitoba: D. W. Friesen and Sons Ltd., 1970), pp. 48-62; Samuel J. Steiner, *Vicarious Pioneer. The Life of Jacob Y. Shantz.* (Winnipeg: Hyperion Press, 1988).

Chapter 37: A Blizzard Baby
This story is excerpted and adapted from "Blizzard," a chapter in Grace H. Kaiser, *Dr. Frau. A Woman Doctor Among the Amish* (Intercourse, Pa.: Good Books, 1986). The story has been condensed from eleven pages in the original. The stories in Kaiser's book are "true," although the author states in an author's note to her book that *Dr. Frau* was written for entertainment and that the names she used are fictitious. Adapted with permission from Good Books.

Chapter 38: The Spear of the Moros
David Hein, ed., *Die Ayoreos—unsere Nachbarn der Mission im noerdlichen Chaco* (Filadelfia, Chaco Paraguay: n.d. [1989?]); Hans J. Wiens, "*Dass die Heiden Miterben seien.*" *Die Geschichte der Indianermission im paraguayischen Chaco* (Filadelfia, Fernheim Chaco, Paraguay: 1989); articles in Mennonite papers such as *Der Bote* and others.

Chapter 39: Shot Down over Germany
H. W. Pankratz, "Road Back Complicated. Living in a German prison camp during the war was humdrum, unpredictable, at times unbearable. Man existed and died in an agony of waiting and life itself was the cheapest commodity of all," *Air Force*, March 1983, pp. 4, 20-21, 24; Letters of Henry Pankratz to me, February 1, 1991, and February 20, 1991. I am grateful to Reuben Epp of Kelowna, British Columbia, for alerting me to this story. I especially thank Henry Pankratz for sending me his published story and graciously answering my questions about aspects of his interesting life.

Chapter 40: Hate and Love
Peter J. Dyck, *A Leap of Faith*. *True Stories for Young and Old* (Herald Press, 1990), pp. 80-110. I am grateful to Peter Dyck and Herald Press for allowing me to adapt this story and for offering valuable suggestions.

Chapter 41: The Battle of the Eyes
Gerhard Woelk, "Der Zwiekampf der Augen," 1972. Handwritten manuscript. Translated and adapted with the author's kind permission.

Chapter 42: Keep It
C. Henry Smith, *The Story of the Mennonites*. Third Edition, revised and enlarged by Cornelius Krahn (Newton, Kan.: Mennonite Publication Office, 1950), pp. 299-315.

Chapter 43: A Courageous Mother
Professor Magdalene Redekop at the University of Toronto encouraged me to write this story about my mother.

Chapter 44: Should George and Anna Evangelize Europe?
For this story the names, except for the author's, have been changed. The story is a composite of several dialogues over years.

Chapter 45: A Conversation on the Train
This story is based on a train ride from Weimar to Mannheim on October 18, 1990. I did not ask for the names of my three fellow travelers, nor did they ask for mine.

The Author

*H*arry Loewen was born in the Ukraine and emigrated to Canada in 1948. After attending Mennonite theological institutions, he studied at such Canadian universities as Waterloo, Manitoba, and Western Ontario, earning B.A., M.A., and Ph.D. degrees. His areas of specialty are Reformation history, German literature, and Mennonite history, literature, and culture.

Loewen taught history and German at a Mennonite high school and at Mennonite Brethren Bible College in Winnipeg, Manitoba (1961-1968). He taught German language and literature and chaired the German department at Wilfrid Laurier University in Ontario (1968-1978). In 1978 Loewen was invited to become the first Chair in Mennonite Studies at the University of Winnipeg. In that position (which he still holds) Loewen developed an academic program in Mennonite studies; taught classes in Mennonite history, culture, and literature; and established, as founding editor, the *Journal of Mennonite Studies*.

Loewen has written or edited several books and published numerous articles and reviews on Mennonite history and literature. Among his eight books are *Goethe's Response to Protestantism* (Herbert Lang, 1972), *Luther and the Radicals* (Wilfrid Laurier University, 1974), *Mennonite Images* (Hyperion Press, 1980), and *Why I Am a Mennonite* (Herald Press, 1988).

A longtime servant of the Mennonite Brethren Church, Loewen takes time to speak and teach in churches and schools. His lectures on Mennonite history and peace issues are especially in demand. One of his main concerns is that Mennonites get to know and appreciate their history and spiritual heritage.

Loewen is married to Gertrude Penner (also from the Ukraine). They are parents of three grown sons—Helmut-Harry, Charles, and Jeffrey. They are also grandparents of Brent and Amber.